the
UNHAPPY
CHILD

the
UNHAPPY
CHILD

what every
parent needs
to know

kenneth n.
condrell, phd

 Prometheus Books
59 John Glenn Drive
Amherst, New York 14228-2197

Published 2006 by Prometheus Books

Inquiries should be addressed to
Prometheus Books
59 John Glenn Drive
Amherst, New York 14228–2197
VOICE: 716–691–0133, ext. 207
FAX: 716–564–2711
WWW.PROMETHEUSBOOKS.COM

10 09 08 07 06   5 4 3 2 1

Library of Congress Cataloging-in-Publication Data

Condrell, Kenneth N., 1937–
     The unhappy child : what every parent needs to know / by Kenneth N. Condrell.
          p. cm.
     Includes bibliographical references and index.
     ISBN 13: 978–1–59102–419–4 (pbk. : alk. paper)
     ISBN 10: 1–59102–419–6 (pbk. : alk. paper)
     1. Child rearing. 2. Child psychology. 3. Parenting. 4. Parent and child. I. Title.

HQ772.C579 2006
649'.1—dc22

                                                              2006008262

Printed in the United States of America on acid-free paper

To my six grandchildren,
Madison, Christopher, Megan,
Hunter, Gabriel, and Amanda.
I know they will touch the lives of many people
during their lifetimes
with their love, compassion, and kindness.

CONTENTS

ACKNOWLEDGMENTS

I wish to acknowledge my wife, Barbara Condrell, who inspired me to share my knowledge of unhappy children with parents and professionals. Barbara read each chapter repeatedly from the perspective of a parent and from the perspective of an editor. Her support and wisdom were invaluable to the manuscript.

Books do not become books without the skills of a talented editor. I wish to thank Steven L. Mitchell, editor in chief of Prometheus Books, for his meticulous attention to the manuscript. I also wish to thank Paul Kurtz, the publisher of Prometheus Books, for giving me the opportunity to have my book published by a company as distinguished as Prometheus.

INTRODUCTION

ersistent unhappiness in a child is a serious symptom. Something is definitely wrong, and the child is reacting. What
is it and how can we find a remedy? Parents intuitively know
this because almost every mother and father I have met
during my forty years of clinical practice has started our first
session by saying, **"Doctor, all I want is for my child to
be happy."**

Children should be happy, vibrant individuals who
explore their world—learning, playing, and having fun. But
no child can expect to enjoy a fulfilling life if his or her days
are overwhelmed with feelings of fear, frustration, anger,
resentment, or other powerful emotions that turn what
should be a special time of life into one of gloomy sadness. In
this book, I will show you how to discover the source of your
child's unhappiness, and I provide many strategies to help you
help your child to be happy again.

If I had one wish, it would be for children to always be
happy, healthy, loved, and cared for. All adults who cherish
children want them to be happy. We want to kiss every hurt

and make it all better. But life can be difficult, and children often do live unhappy lives. As a child psychologist I have been talking and listening to unhappy children for more than four decades. I know that if a child's unhappiness persists, the youngster is at risk for developing serious mental and emotional disorders, even depression.

The American Medical Association reports that mental disorders have become the leading disability among our children, and depression is at the top of the list. A number of studies have reported that upward of 25 percent of US children and 8.3 percent of teenagers suffer from depression. Today more people are experiencing depression earlier in life than in any previous decade. Studies also show that depression in children and adolescents is associated with an increased risk of suicide, which is now the third leading cause of death in young people between the ages of ten and twenty-four (see references).

Why are mental health problems in general and depression in particular on the rise for children and adolescents in the United States? Dr. Nicholas J. Long, a professor of special education at American University in Washington, DC, responds:

> The decay and dysfunction of the family and the shocking social problems in communities have created a new level of deviancy and disturbance never before seen by adults who work with children.

Dr. James Garbarino, Maude C. Clarke Chair in Humanistic Psychology at Loyola University in Chicago, agrees:

I think it is because children today live in a socially toxic environment. What I mean by the term socially toxic environment is that the social world of children, the social context in which they grow up, has become poisonous to their development. The lack of adult supervision and time spent doing constructive, cooperative activities are important toxic aspects of the social environment today, and compound the effects of other negative influences in the social environment for kids. Kids home alone are more vulnerable to every cultural poison they encounter than they would be if backed up by adults.

Knowledgeable people and experts provide us with many reasons for the increase of mental health problems in children. I have my own list of reasons:

- overworked and overscheduled parents who have little time to enjoy a fulfilling family life and for one-on-one time with each child
- parents dismissing their child's troublesome behavior as being either a stage or an attitude problem rather than seeing the behavior as symptomatic of a developing emotional problem
- children unprepared by their parents to cope successfully with life outside of the home
- children growing up in a conflicted, unhappy, tension-filled home environment
- children stressed and overwhelmed by multiple family breakups and remarriages

- children parented by parents with untreated mental health disorders
- peer cruelty and bullying that is so prevalent today in our schools and neighborhoods
- the many opportunities in our society today for children to get into trouble
- the media exposing children to terrible role models who undermine the good intentions of the best parents
- less than 20 percent of the emotionally troubled children in this country receiving treatment

Given the many and enormous obstacles facing children, parents, and families today, I am tremendously encouraged that millions of parents like you are doing a heroic job of raising their children. You would not have purchased this book if your children were not number one in your life. I offer it to help parents just like you. I want to share with parents what I have learned over the years so that my observations about interactions between parents and children can help you recognize your children's unhappiness before it leads to more serious emotional or psychological problems. I will show you how to search for the hidden feelings that plague your unhappy child. Then I will provide practical advice to assist you in your efforts to resolve your child's unhappiness and thereby reduce his or her risk for further emotional distress.

The Unhappy Child: What Every Parent Needs to Know shows you in very practical ways how to help your unhappy child. The first chapter is about divorce. There is a saying that you can take a bad situation and make it worse. Divorce is generally a bad situation for children. This chapter makes parents aware of how they can avoid making their divorce worse for their children. Chapter 2 focuses on how depression can impair a mother's or a father's ability to parent. I show parents how they can become aware of their depression, help themselves, and eventually become effective parents again. In chapter 3 I emphasize how important it is for parents to be vigilant in recognizing the signs that one or more of their children have concluded that they are failures—that they are not as good as other children. Once this destructive feeling is uncovered, I offer parents sound options for reinforcing and stimulating their child's sense of self-worth.

Chapter 4 is about how children suffer when they are without friends. Here I instruct parents on how to guide their child toward attracting more friends and how to protect their son or daughter from the abuse of school bullies. In chapter 5 I offer help to those parents who unknowingly have hurt their children as a result of frequent fights or continuous quarreling. Favoritism is the focus in chapter 6, where I guide parents to understand the harm favoritism brings upon the less-favored child, and I explain in detail what they can do to overcome this problem. In chapter 7 I show parents how their permissiveness not only fails to prepare their children for life's challenges but also creates unruly, undisciplined, and ultimately unhappy children. Parents are offered much-needed advice on how best to take charge of their families.

The problems of stepfamilies are taken up in chapter 8. Parents are provided with a map for wading through all the traps inherent in a blended family and with useful tips on how to achieve the strong familial bonds each member so desperately seeks. Chapter 9 spotlights a topic few parents recognize as a problem at all, namely, sibling abuse. I explain what parents can do to intervene when one child is incredibly cruel to another child in the family. In chapter 10 I show parents how their excessive anger undermines their efforts to parent effectively, and I offer guidance on how mothers and fathers can better manage that anger.

After working through so many of the ordinary and extraordinary causes for unhappiness in today's child, I turn in chapter 11 to a subject that gives me tremendous pleasure and satisfaction. I finally have the opportunity to describe what children need to be happy.

People understandably are cautious about taking advice from someone they do not know, especially where their children are concerned. So let me tell you how my interest in children began. My career goals took shape after a life-changing experience that introduced me to the world of the unhappy child. This experience launched my professional life by teaching me so much about helping these sad kids and what they need to become well adjusted and happy.

When I was a nineteen-year-old college student, I was searching for a career. Becoming a child psychologist had crossed my mind a few times. But, like many students my age, I did not really know much about parenting, and I certainly had no knowledge of how to help troubled children. It was at this point when, out of the blue, a brochure arrived in my mail. It was from the University of Michigan's Department of Psychology. I had not sought any specific information from that university, and to this day I have no idea how the brochure found its way to my door.

The mailer announced that the Department of Psychology was looking for college students with an interest in children to become house parents at a summer camp called the Fresh Air Camp. As I read the brochure, I learned that the university would not only pay me a small salary but also train me to work with troubled children and that I would earn college credit. This opportunity really interested me. It could not have come at a better time. It seemed like just the experience I needed to determine if a career in child psychology was right for me. I immediately filled out the form and applied for the position. In a couple of weeks, the people at the university responded with some tests they wanted me to take. Apparently my responses were satisfactory, because in a few weeks I was accepted to work at the camp. With all the excitement a young man could muster, that summer I drove from my hometown of Buffalo, New York, through Canada, to Ann Arbor, Michigan, and on to the campsite. I remember feeling a great sense of adventure as I drove through the forest and into a clearing that housed the camp. I had no idea that what I was about to experience would change my life forever.

Shortly after I arrived, I met other college students from all over the country, who, like me, had unexpectedly received this brochure. This was such an exciting time. Within hours of my arrival I learned, to my surprise, that the camp was being run by a team of top child psychologists and social workers from throughout the country. I also learned that the camp was part of a research program for troubled children. We were not only there to create a great summer experience for the kids but also to participate in an experiment to see if it was possible to change the lives of sixty unhappy children in just eight short weeks. The camp was also an experiment designed to help prevent unhappy children from growing up to be troubled adults.

The plan was to structure each day with a variety of fun activities to build up each child's self-esteem, while, at the same time, surrounding the children with 120 house parents who by nature were very patient and kind adults. Our professors believed we needed this ratio of two adults for every child to provide the children with the most nurturing environment possible and to teach the children how to get along. This was needed because it was obvious that their social skills were terrible.

A few days after all the student counselors had arrived at the camp, the children arrived. I will never forget that day. Three yellow school buses pulled up to the main lodge of the camp one morning, as we counselors waited outside the lodge. This giant crowd of professors and students was primed and set to welcome these children for a summer of fun. The buses came to a stop, the doors opened, and out came sixty of the most unhappy children I had ever seen in my whole life. They had just arrived at this beautiful camp and, within seconds, they were complaining, pouting, fighting, making abusive statements, and behaving miserably. I felt emotionally overwhelmed. My eyes filled with tears. One of the other college students had been a veteran of the Korean War and, despite his considerable war experience, he, too, became emotional over the sight of these children. I wondered what had happened to these youngsters. Why were they so unhappy?

By the end of that summer I had the answer to my question and I also knew I wanted to be a child psychologist. I returned to this very special camp the following summer, and the summer thereafter. My career was launched by this incredible experience and by the talented faculty who taught me. I went on to become a child psychologist in private practice, and in the forty years that have followed I have talked and listened to thousands of unhappy kids. I have learned what makes children unhappy and what makes them happy. My goal is to share with all parents what I have learned about children and what makes them happy and contented.

WHAT IS GOING ON HERE?

Asking this question is the first step any parent must take in helping his or her unhappy child. I want you to ask yourself this question and, by taking on the attitude of a detective, search for the hidden feelings within your child. As we progress together, you will read descriptions of the ten most undetected causes of unhappiness in children and you will hear kids who have opened up to me and expressed, in their own words, the hidden feelings that have made them so miserable. (I have, however, changed the name of the children to protect their anonymity.) When parents learn the ten causes of deep-seated childhood unhappiness, they are in the best position to discover which of these causes applies to their child and then to rely on the time-tested remedies offered in this book to develop a plan for improving the emotional well-being of their son or daughter.

The following three stories of unhappy children illustrate my approach of first thinking like a detective to discover the source of the child's distress and then treating like a doctor to find a remedy that works to solve the problem.

A father of a very depressed ten-year-old boy once asked me for my help. He was adamant about not following the advice of another psychologist, who suggested that his son take an antidepressant medication. After studying and reviewing his situation, I discovered the problem. I turned to the father and with great concern in my voice said, "I also do not favor giving a young child antidepressants. If you want to avoid medication, you will need to convince your son that you love him." The father looked stunned. I continued, "Your son was once unhappy, but now he is depressed because for years he has believed you don't love him. If you want to see your son's depression disappear, then convince him you love him and that he is special to you." To my surprise, this father rose to my challenge. He didn't get defensive or angry, and he didn't storm out of my office. Instead, he took my advice, which in part included scheduling more overnights with his son. As the quality time he spent with his son increased, the boy's disposition changed dramatically. This bond made all the difference to a son who just wanted his father's love and attention.

A single-parent mom once told me how she went to great lengths and expense to adopt her only child from Vietnam. At the time of our meeting, her little girl was six years old. As I spoke with this woman, she complained about her daughter: "She doesn't behave, Doctor. She doesn't listen to me. She is no fun to be with. She doesn't seem to be a happy little girl." As the history unfolded, I learned that Mom adopted her little girl at the age of one. According to the history, this one-year-old child had spent the first year of her life in an orphanage where a very small staff was overwhelmed by a huge population of abandoned babies. There were no mattresses and no toys and no one to pay attention to these babies. Mom had adopted this child unaware that her new daughter had been emotionally deprived before she brought her to America. Upon returning to this country, this single-parent mom immediately placed her newly adopted year-old daughter in a daycare center for five days a week from 6:30 in the morning to 6:30 at night and returned to her business.

After studying the history, I discovered the problem. This mom had no idea how her decision to rely on daycare so quickly after the adoption further deprived her baby and jeopardized the little girl's ability to bond with her. I responded to this mother with a combination of care and directness. I explained that her daughter doesn't listen, doesn't behave, and is unhappy because she had never fully attached herself to her new mom. I pointed out that she would have to make her daughter a priority over her business and do everything possible to inspire her daughter to bond with her. This mom was very willing to do whatever it took to help her daughter. I recommended that she start by taking her daughter out of daycare and spending more one-on-one time with her child. We then met biweekly for a program of counseling. Within a year this new mom had fostered the connection that was missing between her and her daughter. Her little girl is now happy, thriving, and cooperative, and her mom now feels like a real mom.

A remarried mom with two daughters came to me wondering why her girls were so unhappy following her new marriage. After listening to the history, it was clear: the man she married loved her but had little interest in his stepdaughters. I asked this bewildered mom, "Why did you marry a man who doesn't love your children?" She responded that she didn't think that would be a problem because the children had her love. I explained that children living with a stepparent who shows no interest in them and expresses no affection toward them will quickly feel rejected. I further explained that the experience of rejection makes anyone, and certainly any child, unhappy. Fortunately, this mom and her new husband agreed to family counseling. I started with the father and coached him on how he could form a relationship with both girls. In a few months the mom, her husband, and the girls became a real loving and happy family.

The parents in these brief stories were good people who were at a loss to discover the sources of their children's unhappy states. My help consisted of first acting like a detective to uncover the causes of the unhappiness and then recommending remedies to resolve the underlying problems. Sometimes the problems that result in a child becoming unhappy are caused by some action of the parent(s). Other times the problems are caused by experiences or people outside the family. Regardless of the nature of the problem, it is always up to the adults in a child's life to discover the nature of the problem, determine the proper remedy, and then to apply that remedy.

You don't have to be a rocket scientist to raise successful, happy children. The basic needs of children are not that hard to understand or to fulfill. All it takes is a loving parent, patience, and an understanding of what makes children happy.

REFERENCES

Garbarino, James. *Raising Children in a Socially Toxic Environment.* San Francisco: Jossey-Bass, 1995.

Hoyert, D. L., K. D. Kochanek, and S. L. Murphy. "Deaths: Final Data for 1997." DHHS Publication no. (PHS) 99-1120. *National Vital Statistics Report* 47, no. 19 (1999): 1–104.

Kaye, David L., Maureen E. Montgomery, and Stephen W. Munson. *Child and Adolescent Mental Health.* Philadelphia: Lippincott Williams & Wilkins, 2002.

Kernan, G. L., and M. M. Weissman. "Increasing Rates of Depression." *Journal of the American Medical Association* 261(1989): 2229–35.

Kerns, Lawrence L., and Adrienne B. Lieberman. *Helping Your Depressed Child.* Rocklin, CA: Prima Publishing, 1993.

Long, Nicholas J., and Mary M. Wood. *Life Space Intervention: Talking with Children and Youth in Crisis.* Austin, TX: Pro-Ed, 1991.

Weissman, M. M., et al. "Depressed Adolescents Grown Up." *Journal of the American Medical Association* 281, no. 18 (May 12, 1999): 1707–13.

CHAPTER 1

MISMANAGED DIVORCES

INTRODUCTION

To say that divorce makes children unhappy is an understatement. For a child, the divorce of his parents is catastrophic. For a child, there is no such thing as a "good divorce," as some experts lead us to believe these days. Divorce is a crisis for a family and the absolute worst news a child can ever hear. Sure kids have friends whose parents are divorced, but most youngsters believe divorce will never happen to their family. Here's what one child said to me about her parent's divorce:

> "I think it was good for my parents to get a divorce, but for us kids it was terrible. My life was never the same. When I get married, I'm going to think about what will happen if I ever get divorced and I have kids."

THE PROBLEM

While all divorces leave emotional and psychological damage in their wake, some are far more damaging than others. Some folks quietly mediate their divorce, remain friendly, and go on to raise their children. Others hire powerful attorneys to litigate against their marriage partner for years in the most hateful manner. In between these two extremes are well-meaning parents who, during the divorce process, sometimes lose their way and mismanage their divorce. The "mismanaged divorce" is a phrase I have coined to describe those divorces in which parents, blinded by their own pain, bring unnecessary and excessive amounts of emotional pressure, guilt, fear, and ultimately unhappiness to their children. These children are the very offspring who are the physical representation of their love and devotion for one another.

There are many ways for parents to mismanage their divorce. In this chapter I focus on two patterns of mismanagement that parents often overlook, both of which can cause children to become unhappy. I have chosen these two patterns because, in my experience, parents often are not fully aware of how these parental responses to divorce negatively impact their children in very significant ways.

The Pattern of Overwhelming the Children

It is Saturday evening and Robert is in his bedroom crying. He is nine years old and this is his first evening without his dad. This was an unbelievable day for Robert. The morning started off like any other Saturday morning: he watched cartoons, ate his Oreos, and drank his milk. But by the afternoon Robert had learned his parents were getting a divorce and Dad was moving out. In fact, Dad moved out that day. This was a Saturday Robert would never ever forget as long as he lived. In the span of just a few short minutes, Robert's life had changed forever. After Dad had left the house, Mom came into the family room crying and raging and told Robert what had happened.

"Your father has left us. He doesn't love us any more," she said. It is hard to imagine things getting any worse than this for a nine-year-old boy, but they did. While Mom was crying, she told Robert that Dad had a girlfriend and that he was moving in with her and that Dad's girlfriend had a son who was nine. This was the first day of many, many unhappy days for Robert.

The parents mismanaged their impending divorce by making two serious mistakes. Dad and Mom made the mistake of turning their son's life upside down with too many changes occurring too fast for a child to handle. Mom then made the mistake of trying to turn her son against his father by informing him that Dad no longer loved him. Here is a brief summary of the two mistakes the parents made as they launched their divorce.

The First Mistake

A child or a teen cannot handle hearing his parents are divorcing and then witnessing Dad move out to live with his girlfriend—all in the same day. When children are bombarded with all this information and upheaval in their lives, they can't cope, and they usually are at risk for developing emotional problems such as feeling betrayed, abandoned, and alienated from the parent. When parents decide to divorce, they need to do what they always do, namely, protect their children from harm, most especially the harm that they themselves can cause. In the case of a divorce, this means that a child needs to experience the divorce process gradually and in well-defined steps. I recommend that children first learn that their parents are divorcing. When informing the children, one parent must not put down the other. Instead, the parents should point out that they have problems they cannot solve. Learning about the divorce is trying enough without stressing the children to believe that one parent is breaking up the family. This is followed in a few weeks by the next step, when one parent moves out of the marital home. Then the children begin to experience going back and forth between Dad's place and Mom's place, and they realize they are not going to lose either parent because of the divorce. The final step occurs when the divorce is legal and the parents begin to inform their children that they are dating other people. The boy in this scenario learned in minutes what should have been spread out over a much longer time frame so he could process the changes and adjust to his new family life.

The Second Mistake

The mom in Robert's situation made the serious mistake of telling her son that he is no longer loved by his father. By making this statement, she was manipulating their son to take her side so as to hurt the father as he left the home.

The Pattern of Parental Abandonment

The second pattern I see in a mismanaged divorce is where the dad or mom begins having children with a new partner and makes the new family a priority over the child or children from the first marriage.

THE CHILDREN SPEAK

Let's listen to how one ten-year-old boy expressed his unhappiness to me about the way his dad was valuing his new family over his first family.

> "My dad pays more attention to his new children than to me. He spends most of his time with them, and when I come over, he barely spends time with me. And when we do spend time together, he brings along my new 'brothers.' It seems like he likes them better. He gives them stuff that I would like. He takes care of his second family of kids before he takes care of his first kids and he uses me for their babysitter."

This boy's unhappiness becomes even more painfully clear in the following note he left his mother shortly after talking with me:

Dear Mom,

I'm feeling real depressed over Dad. I can't handle this anymore. I just want to be alone so I'm going into the woods. I will be there for a day or two. Please let me be. I have food and drinks. Don't worry I will be fine.

Bill

———

A six-year-old boy expressed his unhappiness to me about his dad. His father had moved out of the house two months earlier and the parents were in the process of a divorce. When I asked this youngster why he seemed so unhappy, he responded: "I went to my dad's new house last week and I saw some pictures." What pictures did you see, I asked. " Pictures of my dad with a lady and some little kids. They were in his bedroom." He continued talking:

"Later that day the lady and the kids in the picture came over to my dad's place. She has a boy my age and a girl my sister's age. The boy has the same name as mine. We spent the day together. We had fun, but my dad spent most of his time talking to this lady and her kids. Now every time my sister and I are with our dad, she is there with her kids. We never get to spend time with our dad alone and he pays more attention to her kids than to us. When I come home from our visits, I just cry. I love my dad, but I don't want to see him anymore."

———

Here, an eleven-year-old boy talks about his father after his parents' divorce:

> "I had a good life until my parents got divorced and then everything was never the same. I only get to see my dad now once in a while. My mom married Harry. Harry is like my new dad. I don't want Harry. I want my regular dad living with me."

—————

An eight-year-old girl expressed her fear of losing her father as a result of her parents' divorce:

> "I felt torn apart when my parents said they were divorcing. I had all these thoughts buzzing through my head like will I ever see my dad again?"

—————

This seven-year-old girl has similar fears of abandonment:

> "Not only was he leaving my mother, he was leaving me."

—————

Notice how this thirteen-year-old boy talks about how his father has changed since the divorce:

"I don't feel loved anymore. When I come up with ideas to do stuff and to have fun, he doesn't want to do them. He is either with his new wife or sleeping or doing stuff. I feel so angry and so frustrated. The way he ignores me makes me feel like something is wrong with me. I really don't care anymore about anything. I have started being mean to my teacher and my grades have dropped."

———

When a man walks out of his marriage and instantly moves in with another women, he very often inspires rage in his wife. This rage comes back and hurts the children in years to come because the mom who is hurt this way rarely can endorse the father as a good father. The children then end up having to hide their love for their father from their mother. Listen to how some children express their feelings about having to hide their love:

"I don't tell my mom about the fun times I have with Dad because it upsets her."

"I tell my mom that I missed her and that we had no fun because she gets mad when I tell her I had a good time with Dad."

"My mom doesn't want me to call my dad so I have to wait till she's not around."

"I pretend I like Mom more when I'm with Mom; then I pretend I like Dad more when I'm with Dad. Then I have to pretend I like Dad's new girlfriend and Mom's new boyfriend, and Dad's girlfriend's children. I'm always pretending."

I have found that even children as young as three can pick up on their mother's anger toward the father. I recall one mom who was confident she had concealed her feelings from her three-year-old daughter and then was shocked when her child asked her one morning: "How come you no like him?"

SOLUTIONS

If you are a mother reading this chapter, here are some recommendations other mothers have found helpful.

In order for a divorced father to improve his relationship with his children, he first needs to become aware of how his behavior has contributed to their unhappiness. There are several ways for a father to gain this awareness.

- Mom can show Dad the chapter in this book.
- Mom can write Dad a letter that is neither attacking nor accusatory but explains how the children feel.
- Mom can talk with Dad when the children are not around and help him understand how the children feel.
- Mom can meet with a family counselor who then can invite Dad in to discuss why their child or children are so unhappy.

- If it is impossible for Mom to communicate with Dad, then maybe she can find some mutually respected member of the family who can talk with Dad about how the children feel.

Once Dad is aware of the feelings of his children, he then needs to talk with them honestly and openly. Dad can use his own words, of course, but here is one way for him to talk with the children.

"I know why you have been feeling so unhappy and why sometimes you don't want to come over to see me. I really understand now how hard it is for you kids to see me living with other kids. I feel bad that you have been feeling that I don't love you as much anymore. I want you kids to know that I love you very much and you are very special to me. I don't want you to feel left out or that you are second best or that I don't love you. So let's make plans to spend half of our time every month alone just like we use to. Also, I will call you every night after dinner so we can talk a little, and here is my phone number at work and at home so you can call me whenever you want. And the next time we are together, let's make plans about how we are going to spend our private time together. In fact, let's have a family meeting at the end of every month to make plans for the next month."

If you are a father reading this chapter, here are some recommendations other fathers have found helpful.

- When you are with your children from the first marriage and your new marriage, make sure to be sensitive as to how you are attending to all the children. The facial expressions and body language of your children can give you clues when they are feeling left out or slighted. Remember, your children are watching you to see if you favor your new family over your old family.
- Encourage your children to talk with you if ever they are feeling left out or hurt. Let them know that you are not a mind reader and that you can't always tell if something is bothering them. If your child tends to hold back from expressing feelings, it is okay to take the first step in clearing the air. A dad can do this by saying, "You look kind of unhappy today. I wonder if you are feeling left out."
- Make sure to attend school meetings with teachers and watch your children perform at school when they are in plays, in the band, or participating in sports. When children feel insecure about their father, they need proof he really cares. Going to school functions is one way for Dad to demonstrate to his children he really cares and loves them. This can be a real challenge at times for a father when his children have events going on at the same time in different schools. I find it helps for a father to anticipate times like this and to consider two options with his children. One, if possible he can split his time between two school events. Or second, he can be fair by alternating his time between the children. The child who misses out on Dad's presence knows that the next time there is a schedule conflict Dad will be at her school.
- Make sure that birthday celebrations involve some pri-

vate time with your children. Children separated from their dad want their dad all to themselves on special occasions like birthdays.

- Hug your children and tell them you love them. Physically touching a child often works like magic in helping a child to feel loved. Children need to hear over and over again they are loved. No child is too old to be hugged.

- Use your imagination and plan time to play and have fun with your children. Fun and play are totally underestimated by parents as a way to nurture a loving relationship with children. When dads enjoy themselves with their children, children see this as proof of being loved.

- Take photos of your children when you are together and make sure they get copies. Also, make sure some of the photos show all of you together. Put your photos in an album and label this album "Our Family." Family photos help children to relive the good times with Dad. Photos are proof to children that they are special to their parents and are loved.

- Create surprises for your children. Kids love surprises. For example, you might pick up your children and have a couple of kites in the car to go kite flying at the park. Try to pick surprises you know your children will love and that you, too, can enjoy. Kids love picnics, bike rides, fishing, camping, watching a new video, miniature golf, and so on. Surprise your children with a rented video they want to see and popcorn. Sitting close to each other on the couch watching a fun movie promotes a lot of good feelings in children. As you think about what you and your children can do, your list of surprises will grow.

- Don't miss scheduled visits with your children. All children of divorce live with the fear that their parents may abandon them. Missing visits makes children feel anxious about losing their dad. And missed visits cause children to question Dad's sincerity about wanting to be with them and the depth of his love.

- If your child confronts you with criticism that is valid, own up to your mistake. Say, "Yes, I was wrong. I'm sorry I hurt your feelings. Sometimes grown-ups do wrong things when they are upset." An apology at the right time can help melt away a child's anger.

- Sometimes it may be necessary to encourage your child to bring a friend along when he visits with you. A friend can act as a buffer between a child and the father he is angry with. Just bringing a friend can make the idea of going to see Dad more appealing. The invited friend gives your child a greater chance of having some pleasant time with you, which, in turn, builds up trust to help heal the relationship.

- Help your children stay connected to grandparents on both sides of the family. Grandparents are very important to kids. Reaching out to your former in-laws as well as to your own parents helps the children to trust you as really caring about their feelings.

- Whenever possible let your children see you talking with their mother. Even if you have a lot of animosity toward your former wife and have to pretend to be friendly, it is worth the effort. It means so much to children of divorce to see their parents being civil to each other in their presence. It is very painful for children to love parents who continue to show that they disrespect or hate each other.

- By all means, do not look to get revenge on your former wife, and never badmouth her to the children. This kind of behavior by a dad always backfires and the children conclude, "Dad is being mean to Mom." In my experience, children are generally very protective of their mothers. This may not be easy for you to do, especially after you hear from the children that their mom has said some really nasty things about you. When you hear these hateful stories that Mom has related to the kids, take a deep breath and just neutralize them by saying to the children, "Your mom is still upset about the divorce, and when people are angry, they say all sorts of things." Then without being defensive just change the subject.

- Give your children time to get to know you outside of the conflicted marriage you had with their mother. A bad marriage brings out the worst in a man and a woman. Once the divorce has taken place, children get to see their parents in a different light, and it is often a better light. I have often heard children of divorce say, "My dad is a really different guy since the divorce. He's nicer and calmer."

- See a child psychologist and a family counselor if you feel really stuck with your children. Sitting down and reviewing the problems you are having with an expert can often be very helpful in finding new ways to improve the relationship you have with your child or children. Over the years, I have guided many men who were estranged from their children. I actually coached them on how to respond to their children's hurt and anger and how to reach out to their children. Very often I would later meet with the children without Dad so as to appreciate their feelings, and then I would have joint sessions so Dad and the children could talk things over. This doesn't always work, but it certainly is worth a try when a father feels helpless in knowing what to do next to help his children be loving and happy with him. The same approach is helpful for mothers who are estranged from their children.

SUMMARY

There are times in the lives of couples when there is no alternative but divorce. The way parents manage their divorce is critical to the happiness of their children. As you can see from my recommendations, I believe it is possible for a dad to have two sets of children and still stay happily connected to all of them. It isn't easy, but it can be accomplished. Every good father wants a loving and happy relationship with his children.

RESOURCES

If you would like to learn more about how you can help your children and yourself, I recommend the following books:

Be a Great Divorced Dad, by Dr. Kenneth N. Condrell with Linda Small (New York: St. Martin's, 1998).

Between Two Worlds: The Inner Lives of Children of Divorce, by Elizabeth Marquardt (New York: Crown, 2005).

Chicken Soup for the Father's Soul: Stories to Open the Hearts and Rekindle the Spirits of Fathers, by Jack Canfield and Mark Victor Hansen (Deerfield Beach, FL: Health Communications, 2001).

Divorced Dad's Survival Book: How to Stay Connected with Your Kids, by David Knox, PhD, with Kermit Leggett (Boston: Perseus Books, 2000).

Getting Divorced without Ruining Your Life, by Sam Margulies, PhD, JD (New York: Simon & Schuster, 1992).

Helping Children Survive Divorce: What to Expect; How to Help, by Archibald D. Hart, PhD (Dallas, TX: World Publishing Group, 1996).

The Involved Father: Family-Tested Solutions for Getting Dads to Participate More in the Daily Lives of Their Children, by Robert Frank, PhD, with Kathryn E. Livingston (New York: St. Martin's, 1999).

Making Divorce Easier on Your Child: 50 Ways to Help Children Adjust, by Nicholas Long, PhD, and Rex Forehand, PhD (New York: Contemporary Books, 2002).

Raising Boys without Men: How Maverick Moms Are Creating the Next Generation of Exceptional Men, by Peggy Drexler, PhD, with Linden Gross (Emmaus, PA: Rodale, 2005).

CHAPTER 2

DEPRESSED PARENTS

INTRODUCTION

Depression is a terrible thing. It sneaks up on you without much notice, so you don't even realize that you're becoming depressed. At first you feel a little blue—not quite yourself. Gradually the blues and the sad days build up and, before you know it, you're experiencing depression. It is estimated that there are about nineteen million Americans who experience some form of depression in their lives. Most people can tell when they are feeling sad, but out of these millions of people, only one-third actually know they are depressed. Many others are not even aware of the terrible things depression can do to a person. They don't know that depression can make a person:

- lose confidence
- feel worthless
- feel tired
- lose interest in having fun

- withdraw from people
- think mostly sad thoughts like not living anymore
- feel like not doing anything
- lose interest in sex
- overly focus on problems and not on what is right about his or her life

Since many people do not know how serious depression can be, they just hope it will go away; they try to tough it out. This is particularly true of men, who typically do not seek help on their own. Usually a man's wife or girlfriend pushes him into getting help. Women are generally more in touch with their feelings and therefore are more likely to both recognize that a problem exists and ask for help in resolving the problem. I know this statement can be interpreted as unfair to men. There are always exceptions to generalities, and not all men are struggling to be in touch with their feelings. However, my colleagues and I have observed that over 90 percent of the calls to our offices for help are made by women. And they almost always bring in a reluctant husband or companion. Millions of people put off getting help for their depression. This is really unfortunate for the person and his or her family, because if there is one emotional disorder we know how to treat better than all the rest, it is depression. In the last twenty years psychiatry and psychology have made remarkable progress in treating depression. Celebrities like musician Billy Joel, reporter Mike Wallace of *60 Minutes*, and former vice president Al Gore's wife, Tipper, have spoken openly about their own bouts with depression. People no longer have to feel ashamed to say, "I'm depressed."

THE PROBLEM

While depression in and of itself is a serious psychological problem, it can become even more pronounced for parents who shoulder the added responsibility of caring for youngsters. Parents set the tone for the entire family. If one or both parents experience depression, the entire atmosphere at home is affected and the children are sure to suffer. When a parent becomes depressed, she becomes difficult for children in the house to live with. She appears boring and no fun for the children. The parent can find it extremely difficult to go on giving of herself and behaving in a loving way. She comes across as negative, critical, and not supportive, as well as irritable and easily frustrated. This is why it is so important for parents to recognize when they are depressed and to seek treatment.

Mothers are especially at a high risk for becoming depressed. Today's mothers are often overworked and overextended. Some mothers also feel trapped without the support of an involved partner. In most families Mom is the glue that holds the group together. She's the one who nurtures the children. In saying this, I'm not being unkind to men. I'm just describing what goes on in the vast majority of households. In most homes, *Mom is it!* And when Mom is depressed, the whole family suffers. I remember seeing a T-shirt that read in large letters, "IF MAMA AIN'T HAPPY, NOBODY'S HAPPY." There is plenty of truth in this statement. A depressed mom can really stress out her family.

Since women are more likely than men to read a book that discusses depression and since mothers are more likely to recognize depression in themselves or their husbands (or male partners), I am directing this chapter to mothers.

Depression can make a mom feel like a failure in life. It robs her of self-worth and makes her confidence level drop to virtually nothing. Depression also makes a mom feel hopeless and pessimistic, as if there are no solutions to the challenges she faces and nothing will ever get better. Depressed mothers often suffer in silence as they lose the ability to enjoy life. Once depressed, a mom will become despondent and withdrawn. In such a state, she is unable to find the energy to care for her children adequately. Often she becomes passive and indifferent. Not only is there a lack of affection and fun, from the point of view of her children, but she has less energy to enforce the rules. Discipline goes out the window. As the children begin to misbehave in response to her lack of discipline and in reaction to her depression, a vicious cycle starts. The children add to Mom's depression by misbehaving and not listening. Clearly, a depressed mom has a terrible time functioning as a parent.

THE CHILDREN SPEAK

A nine-year-old girl expressed her unhappiness to me about her depressed mom:

> "My mom is always sad. She started drinking and my dad doesn't know how to get her to stop. I hear them fighting at night. It's like I don't have a family any more. I hate my life. I feel like running away."

———

An eight-year-old boy voiced concern and unhappiness about his depressed mom:

> "Sometimes I sit in school and just daydream and worry about my mom. It seems like she doesn't love me any more. She doesn't play with me any more. All she does is complain. My mom used to be fun."

———

The effect of depressed fathers can be equally devastating to children, as this eleven-year-old boy showed when he talked with me about what his life was like with his single-parent dad.

> I started my session with Karl by asking him how the drive was to the office, since it was snowing. "Okay," he said.
>
> "What did you and your dad talk about on the way in," I asked.
>
> "Nothing."
>
> I responded by saying, "Karl, the drive from your house to my office takes seventy-five minutes. You and your dad must have had a conversation."
>
> Karl looked at me and said, "My dad didn't talk."
>
> "You just showed me your report card. It is the best card you ever had. What did your dad say when he saw your card?" I asked.
>
> "Nothing."

"You mean, your dad not only didn't talk with you in the car but said nothing to you about your report card?"

"That's right. And what really bothers me is the way he walks into the kitchen or living room where I'm sitting and says nothing. It's like I'm not there."

"Have you and your dad done any fun things lately," I asked?

"Nope."

Karl's father had brought his son in to see me initially because he was refusing to help out at home and had stolen some junk food from a corner deli. I knew his father was depressed from the moment I first met him. What was so amazing is that this dad knew there was a problem with his son. He was willing to drive over an hour so I could see the boy and he also was very willing to pay my fee. But the father had no idea he was depressed and that his behavior was generating a lot of resentment in his son. Depressed parents often make their children feel unloved and not special. When children feel deprived, they often respond with anger and begin to behave in angry ways.

I have listened to so many children complain over the years about life with a depressed parent. That is why I believe it is so important for mothers to become aware of their depression and to look for solutions.

If you recognize yourself in this chapter, the following

solutions can help you to both improve your life at home and help your unhappy child.

SOLUTIONS

1. Explain to Your Children That Your Mood Is Not Their Fault

Children personalize their experiences with parents. This means if Mom is sad and gloomy, her children will conclude that they did something to make her feel that way. They will feel it is their fault. One of the first things you should do is to inform your children that they did not make you sad. This will help your children to not blame themselves for making you unhappy. Here is one way to explain things to your child.

> "You know Mommy has not been feeling well lately. I have been feeling very tired and sad. I just want you to know that this is not your fault. Since I look sad and I haven't played with you much lately, you might think I'm mad at you and that you have done something bad to make me feel so sad. It is not you at all. I will be getting better in a few months. I just want you to know I love you very much. And promise me, if you think I am mad at you, just ask me and we can talk about how we are feeling."

2. Make Some Free Time for Yourself

Mothers have a tendency to always put their needs last. Though this is admirable, a mother can easily burn herself out by setting aside her own adult interests as well as her need to be alone. Spending time away from the children is very important. It will give Mom a chance to "recharge her battery." It will also help her to deal more effectively with her depression.

When I lecture I tell parents, "Do your children a favor by getting away from them." One depressed mom related to me how she arranged a whole day to herself. She went to a popular bookstore in town, bought a cup of coffee, and read an entire book. It had been years since she had spent that kind of time on her own, enjoying a good book, and it made her feel wonderful. For this particular mom, reading a book while relaxing away from her three children was the best medicine. So, I say to all mothers, and especially those who might be suffering from depression, rely on your partner or relatives or friends or a sitter to carve out some private adult time for yourself. A good part of your depression comes from feeling deprived.

3. Family Meetings Can Strengthen Relationships with Your Children

Family meetings can help Mom improve those all-important emotional bonds with her children. Such meetings bring all the members of a family together, parents and children, and are scheduled weekly or biweekly. Some families also allow for the scheduling of spur-of-the-moment meetings when there is a crisis, a significant event has occurred, or one is coming up.

There are many benefits to a family coming together regularly for its scheduled meeting. At the top of this list of benefits is the building of stronger family relationships and a greater sense of loyalty on the part of the children toward the parents. I have counseled thousands of families and have noticed during the last twenty years that lack of family loyalty is one of the biggest problems parents face today. When children feel valued and wanted by their parents, they feel a special connection with their family. This special connection is what I mean by *loyalty*. I believe that busy families have found themselves relying on multiple caregivers for the children, and this has left many children feeling distant from their parents and with a weak sense of what *family* is all about. Holding family meetings is a great way to help children feel connected to their parents and strengthen loyalty to their family. There are also other benefits to holding family meetings such as:

- Children feel more motivated to cooperate.
- The role of the parents as the leaders of the family is strengthened, thus promoting a sense of security in the children.
- Children learn and appreciate the importance of talking things over.
- Children feel they are an important and valued members of the family because they *contribute* to the running of the family.

I recommend that parents rely on the following guide for holding a family meeting:

- Schedule the meeting when the family can be relaxed and not rushed.
- Plan on fifteen to twenty minutes per meeting.
- Hold the meeting at a table with chairs for everyone.
- Children from the age of three years and up should participate.
- State the rules for the family meeting: for example, no interrupting, no arguing, and everyone will have the chance to speak. And be prepared to listen to what your children have to say.
- Open the meeting with a short and simply worded review of how the family has been doing since the last meeting. It's important to be positive and to offer compliments for cooperation and for contributing to the success of the previous meeting.
- Clearly state the purpose of the current meeting by outlining its agenda—what exactly will be discussed. Make sure your agenda always includes free time at the end for all members to bring up issues, concerns, and problems they have feelings about.
- Close the meeting with a fun family experience such as making popcorn or playing a game.

Here are some tips to facilitate your family meetings:

- Help your children to know you have really heard and appreciate how they feel by putting their ideas and concerns in your own words. For example, you might say to your child after he complained about his bedtime,

"So, you think you should have a later bedtime since you are the oldest."

- Take a problem-solving approach in your family meetings so all the members will come to realize that improvements are taking place as a result of the meetings. For instance, to a child who wants a later bedtime, a parent might respond: "I agree that you are the oldest and should have a later bedtime, but you also are the hardest one to wake up in the morning. How about trying out a later time for one week, but it will be up to you to get yourself up. If you can get yourself up when your alarm clock goes off in the morning, you can have the later bedtime."

- Encourage your children to speak up and express themselves, and be careful not to judge what they say. They may be your children, but they are also individuals who should be respected for having their own opinions. Parents sometimes respond to children's feelings by listing many reasons why the children shouldn't feel the way they do. Avoid this common way of responding to children and instead invite your children to go on telling the family their side of things. This can build much-needed confidence in the youngsters, and they will respect you for hearing them out.

- As you listen to your children, listen for themes that underlie their concerns or complaints.

- Ask questions in the family meetings that help inspire the children to feel proud of their family. For example, you might ask:

"What's good about being in our family? Why are you glad you are in this family?"

"Does anyone have something nice to say to anyone or want to say thank you to anyone?"

"Dad and I need help making plans for Thanksgiving this year. Do you have any ideas?" Or say, "Mom and I need your help to solve a problem."

- Use a large calendar you can buy at an office supply store along with magic markers to write down all the plans that have been agreed upon at the family meetings. This will make it easy for all the members of the family to see what is coming up. A calendar also makes it more likely that family plans will not be forgotten or put off.
- Plan an event for after the family meeting that the children can look forward to. For example, you might say:

"Let's have our meeting first and then watch the movie we rented."

"As soon as our family meeting is over, we will all go out for ice cream."

"At the end of our meeting today, we will make popcorn and play a family game."

Depressed parents often distance themselves from their children. They withdraw into themselves. Family meetings can really help a depressed parent communicate to the children that Mom or Dad is close and does care for them. Feeling wanted, valued, and desired is very important to all of us, but especially to children. If you have an unhappy child because of your depression, then regular family meetings are a must.

4. Change Your Attitude about Problems in Life

It is very possible that you are depressed because of some unexpected setbacks in your life. If this explains your depression, then you may need to examine your attitude about life and change the way you have been thinking about problems. Negative, pessimistic thoughts feed a depression. Here are some tips on how to change your attitude in order to minimize your negative thoughts and pessimistic outlook when trouble strikes.

The first step toward changing your outlook on life is to recognize and accept that life is difficult. Not only is life difficult, but that elusive happiness we all seek is not a continuous state of mind. Sometimes we're happy and sometimes we're not. Sometimes we feel in control of our lives and sometimes we feel like we have totally lost control. Sometimes we are having fun and sometimes life hurts so much that we feel like we want to die. Sometimes we advance our lives and sometimes we experience setbacks.

I really believe that "it is not what happens to us in life that is so important but how we think about what has happened to us." Therefore, your new attitude about life should be one of expecting to experience setbacks and problems. You need to think of yourself as a problem solver. With this new attitude that *setbacks and problems are to be expected*, you are in a position of strength to cope, to survive, and to solve your problems.

Setbacks happen to everyone, rich or poor, to the famous and to the not so famous, to the educated and to the not so well educated. All we have to do is look to the media to find proof of this observation. We turn on the TV and learn that the home of a factory worker burned to the ground on Christmas Eve or we learn that the son of a celebrity was murdered. We pick up a newspaper and learn of a local young man who died from an overdose. And then we hear about famous actors like Ed Asner or Mary Tyler Moore losing a child to drugs. Life does not spare anyone. There are all sorts of setbacks in life. These may affect your finances, your career, your marriage, your parenting, your relationships, your health, or any number of other aspects of your life.

When we experience setbacks in life, our immediate response is almost always one of shock and feeling overwhelmed. We are in a stage of disbelief soon to be followed by a stage of grief and despair. We come to feel sorry for ourselves, and for a while we feel lost, hurt, confused, and powerless. As the weeks and months pass, we either settle on feeling victimized by life or we take on the attitude of *setbacks are to be expected. Bad things happen to good people all the time. Now what?* Many celebrities go on with their lives. I personally saw Bill Cosby perform after his son's murder. He had the audience members falling out of their chairs with laughter though in his heart he was still grieving the loss of his son.

Life will go on after a terrible event, and the only person who can decide how it will go on is *you*. World-renowned cyclist Lance Armstrong survived cancer in 1999 and went on to win the Tour de France six more times.

5. Read Inspiring Stories

Many people have found it helpful to read inspiring books about those who have faced adversity and made a comeback. Inspiring stories about famous and not-so-famous people can encourage us not to give up and to go forward with our lives. The comedian Joan Rivers has a set of audiocassettes worth listening to. On these tapes she describes her return to show business after her husband committed suicide. Not only did Joan lose her husband, but no one would hire a comedian who just became a widow. Agents concluded, "A grieving widow just can't be funny. Besides, who is going to come out to listen to a comedian whose husband just killed himself?" Joan's story about her comeback is very inspiring. So is the story of Christopher Reeve, who was left paralyzed after a horse-riding accident. Although he was unable to move, he traveled, made public presentations, raised money, and gave a voice to all those who are paralyzed. In an interview, Reeve revealed that he spent twenty minutes each day crying and then went on to live each day as fully as possible. Skater Scott Hamilton's life offers every reader inspiration. A four-time world figure skating champion, Scott's career was interrupted by testicular cancer. He responded by turning his career into an opportunity to help others. Scott now lives with the vision of helping to eradicate cancer within his lifetime. His statement "the only disability left is a bad attitude" is a valuable lesson for all who are struggling with some adversity.

I personally know a teacher who gave birth to two sons. Both boys were born deaf. After grieving her lost dream of having normal, hearing children, this mother, who was quite depressed, quit her job and devoted herself to teaching her boys to speak. The method she created for teaching her sons to speak resulted in her being honored years later at the Kennedy Center in Washington, DC. Thousands of parents are grateful to this woman and the school she developed to help children cope with the adversity of deafness.

I know a man who lost his job as a truck driver because of an accident that left him disabled. To help pay his bills, he went door to door selling his wife's pies. In a few short years this man grew his business to a level where he sold pies to the major restaurant chains in New York State.

Setbacks, as you see, can at times be hidden opportunities to change our lives. I personally have helped many married couples who were struggling to deal with the devastating effects of an affair and who were on the verge of divorce find ways to save their marriages. The affairs opened their eyes to what was wrong in their marriages. They worked hard to overcome these obstacles in their relationships and went on to have lives together filled with true companionship and real intimacy.

The question is, how are you going to deal with the setbacks in your own life? Here is some of the best advice I have learned over the years.

- Seek out a professional counselor, life coach, or expert to help you examine your life and to develop a plan to cope with your setback or problem. A plan is a powerful tool for moving yourself from a position of helpless passivity to one of making things happen in your life. If you have declared bankruptcy, a professional accountant can help you to develop a plan to better handle your money problems, establish credit, and get on with your life. If your marriage ended in divorce, a counselor can help you to see that divorce is another chance at finding the right person for yourself. If you can't have children, a professional who guides parents to adopt can assist you to become the parent you always wanted to be. If you are physically sick, a second and third medical opinion could well turn something up that might help you recover.

- Nurture a circle of friends who are positive, upbeat, and really like you. Relationships are so very important in changing our lives after a setback. Women especially respond better to their depression when they are socially connected to other women.

- Make a list of what is right about your life. At the top of this list, write down that you are an American citizen. Make note of this because it will remind you that you live in one of the few countries in the world where you are free to create your own life. Most of my relatives were poor, uneducated immigrants who came to this country and created wonderfully rich lives for themselves.

- Remind yourself that in life you have to be a problem solver. Life is filled with problems. Expect problems, anticipate them, and deal with them.

- Make a list of affirmations and read them every day.

Affirmations are statements that you recite to place yourself in a positive frame of mind. They help you keep focused and dedicated to changing your life. Some affirmations are:

This terrible time in my life is temporary.

I will survive and move my life forward.

I must think of my goals every day.

I have survived in the past and I will survive this setback.

- Dream your dreams. Every person I have talked to who has a meaningful life has said to me, "Dream your dreams and you will be living them." The secret is, "As you think, so shall you be." Your mind is your most powerful asset for changing your life. Take lessons on how to relax, focus, and visualize the changes you want to make.
- Ask yourself, "Is there anything good about this awful experience I am going through?" My own success as a child psychologist and family therapist never would have happened if I had not been fired from the second job I had. I was and I expected to be a professor for the rest of my life. After feeling devastated and ashamed by the loss of this position, I found my true purpose in life. Adversity can sometimes offer opportunities we never dreamed of.

6. Learn the Basics about Depression

Here is basic information you need to know to help yourself with your depression:

- Doctors today are more familiar with depression than ever before. Your family doctor can help you to determine if you have a depression by administering a short screening test. He then may decide to treat you or possibly refer you to a psychiatrist.
- Recognize that there is often a chemical component to your depression. This means most likely that you will need medication to balance out your body chemistry in order to relieve your depression. I have heard people refer to antidepressants as "happy pills." Antidepressants are not happy pills. They do not make you happy. What they do is help balance out your body chemistry so that the depression subsides. It helps to think of an antidepressant as if it were a vitamin. It is something your body needs to make your nervous system work better. Today more than ever before, psychiatry has some very effective medications for depression with limited side effects. Your doctor will decide what is best for you.
- You need to know that most doctors start patients off with a small dose and then gradually increase the medication until the right level is reached. The right level is when you are feeling better with hardly any side effects.
- Sometimes a person will have a negative reaction to a prescribed antidepressant and give up on antidepressants altogether. A better approach is to talk with your doctor

so that you can switch to another medication that will work better with your system.

- Antidepressants are not like taking aspirins. You don't take one and start to get results within an hour. Antidepressants need to build up in your system. So you may not feel the results right away.

- What can you expect from an antidepressant? You can expect to have your moods stabilize and to have fewer mood swings. You can expect that you will not be thinking over and over again about all the things that are not right in your life or in the world. And you can expect to feel more energetic and to be more positive.

- Should you just treat a depression only with medication? The answer is no. You need to receive counseling in order to handle the events that triggered the depression. A depression is often a signal that something is not right in your life. Medication helps you to have the energy to tackle your problems through counseling.

SUMMARY

If you think you are a mom with a depression, then do yourself and your family a favor. Start following the suggestions in this chapter and consider getting some help for yourself. It's normal to feel the blues and it's normal to feel sad from time to time, but when week after week passes and you feel despair and gloom and you hate getting out of bed, then you need to ask for help. As you improve and your mood brightens, the feelings and attitude of your unhappy child will also improve.

RESOURCES

If you would like to learn more about your depression and how it affects the well-being of your child, I recommend the following books and Web site:

How Did I Get Here? Finding Your Way to Renewed Hope and Happiness When Life and Love Take Unexpected Turns, by Barbara De Angelis (New York: St. Martin's, 2005).

How to Stop Worrying and Start Living, by Dale Carnegie (New York: Pocket Books, 1944).

I Can't Get Over It: A Handbook for Trauma Survivors, by Dr. Aphrodite Matsakis (Oakland, CA: New Harbinger Publications, 1996).

The Impossible Just Takes a Little Longer: Living with Purpose and Passion, by Art Berg (New York: Quill, 2002).

Worry, Hope, and Help for a Common Condition, by Edward M. Hallowell, MD (New York: Random House, 1977).

Your Erroneous Zones, by Dr. Wayne Dyer (New York: Avon Books, 2001).

http://www.depression.com

CHAPTER 3

CHILDREN WHO FEEL LIKE FAILURES

INTRODUCTION

Over the years I have counseled many children who for various reasons saw themselves as failures in life. These children believe there is something wrong with them. They feel different from other children, and the difference they perceive is definitely negative.

Some of these children feel different because of their looks. They may not possess what many people perceive as standard good looks or they aren't attractive in some other way. They are not cute kids like those we see in toy and breakfast cereal commercials. Their nerdy or unusual looks stand out, and often they are teased by other children. "Dumbo ears," "giraffe neck," and "butt head" are just some of the names they endure. Some of the children I counsel feel different because they are physically awkward, overweight, and clumsy. Skipping, running, throwing, catching, and riding a bike—all quite normal activities for most children—are more difficult for these youngsters to master. These kids have poor coordination, which makes it difficult for them to play successfully with other children. Play-time, when you're a child, requires physical coordination, and when you are far from coordinated, you stand out. Some of these children feel different because they have handicaps such as cerebral palsy, seizures, or a limp. Some may be missing a limb or are blind or deaf.

The one group of children whose members, in my opinion, suffer the most, though, is a group whose difference is invisible to others. These children do not have a disability that is obvious to parents. The children I'm referring to are slow learners. These children suffer every day as they struggle to survive in a school system designed for children who learn at an average to above-average level.

THE PROBLEM

When children can't compete with others in their age group, or they can't perform well within a group of their peers, they become unhappy. Such youngsters become painfully unhappy because their daily experiences chip away at their self-esteem and their self-confidence. It is next to impossible to be a happy child when self-esteem and self-confidence are lacking. *Self-esteem* is the reputation a child has with himself. It is how he feels about himself as he compares himself with other children. Whereas adults can strive to be self-accepting, children generally measure themselves against their peers. *Self-confidence* refers to how competent a child perceives himself to be. A self-confident child feels secure in knowing he can do things. Children who perceive themselves and who are perceived by their peers to be different in some negative way struggle with low levels of self-esteem and self-confidence.

Slow learners in particular have a very hard time maintaining adequate levels of self-esteem and self-confidence. These children often are reported to have average intelligence. However, if we look carefully at their IQ scores, we discover that they score at the *bottom* of the average range of intelligence. This label of *average* is technically correct but misleading; it misleads these children, their parents, and their teachers to expect that they can do better in school than they are at present. The parents think their children are average; teachers respond to these youngsters as if they are average; and the children themselves think they should learn as fast as everyone else. But they can't. The reality is that these children are not average learners, and each year they fall further and further behind in school. Generally, these children are at the bottom of their class. And by fourth grade they are about two grade levels or more behind everyone else in reading, spelling, math, and writing.

When I meet these slow-learning children in my office, my heart goes out to them. They usually are the nicest kids but so unhappy because they can't keep up with their classmates. Imagine yourself going to work every day and performing at a level that is the poorest level at your place of employment. You look around and see everyone ahead of you doing their work faster, easier, and better. In time you come to feel ashamed of yourself. You come to feel dumb. You come to see yourself as a failure. Now you know what it's like to be a slow learner. Children who are slow learners just can't meet the expectations they have for themselves or the expectations others have for them. Is it any wonder, then, why these children are unhappy? Parents often have no idea why their below-average child is so unhappy. When parents consult me, they frequently report that their child hates school, is lazy, or is an underachiever and lacks motivation. Almost always the message the parents communicate to me is one of being hugely disappointed with their child.

If we put ourselves in the shoes of the slow learners, we see what they are up against. Their parents are disappointed with them and often annoyed. Their brothers and sisters or their school friends are often passing them by in class. Their teachers are disappointed and often frustrated with them. And the kids are disappointed with themselves; they feel frustrated because they see other children outperforming them and they sense the disappointment from the adults with whom they are very close and to whom they look for encouragement, support, and approval.

Many years ago, when I was a young child psychologist, I used to go skiing with a pediatric neurologist. We both had busy practices. Many of the children referred to us were slow learners. One evening we went to our group skiing class and somehow accidentally found ourselves in the advanced class. Since it was too late to find our intermediate class, we decided to stay with this more-advanced group. The experience was awful. We couldn't keep up. We kept falling and making mistakes and holding everyone back. In a short time we were feeling pretty inadequate. Finally, the experience became so embarrassing that, when no one was looking, we skied away into the darkness without anyone seeing us. When we reached the bottom of the mountain, we both looked at each other and laughed. There we were, two doctors who were known as experts in the community on kids with learning problems, behaving just like the kids we saw every day. We stopped trying to learn, gave up, and avoided the class altogether. The big difference between us and the kids we counseled was that we had lots of other successes in our lives and we didn't have to face this skiing class every single day. This experience really gave us more compassion for our young clients who almost always hated school.

THE CHILDREN SPEAK

There are many slow learners who never speak up. They are often shy and ashamed. It's as though they have this deep, dark secret about themselves—that they really are dumb—and by not speaking they can somehow hide this perceived fact about themselves from those around them. These children are terrified that others will say what they are pretending isn't so: that they are dumb. Many of the slow learners I see in my practice cannot talk about their feelings, but their parents speak for them. I remember a mother of a ten-year-old boy who said to me:

> "Robert never complains, but his body language speaks volumes. You can just see in the morning how he dreads going to school. As he walks to the school bus stop, he is hunched over looking like his best friend died. Every morning is like this. When he comes home, Robert looks exhausted. Every day he

falls on the couch after school and sleeps for two hours. He loves Fridays because there is no school the next day, but Sunday nights are terrible for Robert. He knows tomorrow starts another week. My poor son is never happy and I just don't know how to help him."

———

A man I know recently told me how hard school was for him as a kid. He told me that he never spoke up as a kid because he felt he was the dumbest one in school. He remembered overhearing his teacher once telling his parents that she considered him a slow learner. And then this man smiled and told me about how he daydreamed in school that Elizabeth Taylor would knock on the classroom door and introduce herself to the teacher as his friend. As he related the daydream, he recalled how, for a few minutes in this fantasy, he felt important because a famous person was his friend, and that all the kids admired him from that day on. "Can you believe that?" he asked me. "Liz Taylor, a world-famous actress, was my friend and she just stopped by to say hello and to see if she could take me out of class for lunch. I can't remember how many times I dreamed that daydream, maybe a thousand times." Then I asked him, "Harry, if you really are a slow learner, how did you achieve all your success? You are a wealthy man." Harry answered, "I worked fifty times harder than any of the other kids and I got through high school. And you want to know something? Even though I'm a success and I'm rich, I still feel inadequate, because I never could handle college." As I listened to this man recall his childhood years, I was reminded how the hurts from our childhood often can last a lifetime even when we have achieved remarkable success as adults.

———

I remember talking to an eight-year-old girl in my office once. She was so quiet and she had this frightened look on her face. Her name was Carol. And Carol was anything but assertive. She waited for me to ask a question before she talked. Carol never just spontaneously spoke up. She was such a sweet kid. She was sensitive, caring, thoughtful, and well mannered. I liked being with her.

As the interview proceeded, it was easy to see how Carol worried about being a good girl and about doing the right thing. But Carol also had a very sad expression on her face. I asked her, "Carol, what is the matter? You look so sad."

Carol responded, "Nothing."

"Oh, but I think something is bothering you. You know I'm a feeling doctor. I help lots of kids. Why don't you tell me, Carol, what's wrong."

Carol, who was staring down at her lap, looked up at me. I now could see tears in her eyes. She said, "I'm a retard."

"What do you mean, you're a retard?" I asked.

"That's what the kids call me," Carol answered.

"Why would they call you a name like that?" I asked.

"Because . . . because I keep failing tests in class, and when the teacher calls on me I'm confused about what the answer should be. My sister and brother are on the honor role and my parents tell me I have to repeat the grade this year. I can tell how disappointed my parents are with me. I think my parents wish they never had me."

By the time Carol expressed all these feelings, I had tears in my eyes. I felt angry. Once again I was seeing a really nice kid, a youngster who should be enjoying her childhood, suffering from shame and confusion because the school she attended was pushing her through an academic program designed for average and above-average kids. The real problem is not Carol and other kids like Carol. The real problem rests with schools that keep functioning as though millions of kids like Carol don't exist. We push these children through an educational meat grinder that leaves them feeling ashamed, miserable, and inferior to their friends and classmates. And then we blame them for not trying harder.

———

I remember talking with another very unhappy eight-year-old girl, named Marie. She, too, was a slow learner and also was missing two fingers on her left hand due to a birth injury. A week earlier, Marie had told her parents she didn't want to live any more. She refused to tell them anything more. The threat of suicide frightened the parents. So I found myself sitting across from this lovely little girl wondering what was going on.

I asked, "Marie, why do you want to die?"

"Because I'm ugly and stupid."

Then she asked me a question I will never forget: "Do you think anyone will ever marry me?"

Once again, I felt like crying. These poor kids suffer so much in our society when they are intellectually at the low end of the average range of intelligence.

———

Over the years, I have learned a lot about slow learners and how to help them survive, thrive, and succeed in life. What follows are my solutions to a problem that has been devastating children for many generations.

SOLUTIONS

1. Accept Your Child for Who He Is

The most important step all parents can take to help their slow learner is to accept their child for what he is. All children in a family are different. Their looks are different. Their temperaments are different. Their talents and interests are different. Their learning styles are different. Parents need to recognize the differences among and between their children, and most do. In fact, many parents will often joke about how it is hard to believe their kids all came from one family. Parents are generally good at adjusting their parenting to deal with the different temperaments of each of their children. But all too often parents fall short when it comes to accepting that one or more of their children is a slow learner. The child who is a slow learner can't help but suffer with low self-esteem as he compares himself to other children. Parents can nurture their slow learner's self-esteem by *fully accepting their child* for the unique individual he is. This acceptance is a powerful experience for a child because no one is more important to a child than his parents.

Parents naturally want their children to be successful, and when they learn that a child in the family has fallen short of expectations, they experience a profound sense of loss. Many parents go through a period of grieving, not unlike that following a death in the family. Sometimes the loss is felt so profoundly that parents have actually fired the psychologist or counselor who informed them that their child shows signs of being a slow learner. Occasionally, parents, in their disbelief at such news, will seek out the professional opinion of psychologist after psychologist looking for that one expert who will tell them what they want to hear—that their child doesn't have a problem.

Eventually, after a time of grieving and feeling distressed over the news that their child is a slow learner, many parents begin the process of accepting their child for who he is. They accept that their child is going to need more time to learn, more time to think, more time to practice, and more extra help with school. Let me say this again because this last statement really defines what a slow learner is all about. Slow learners are going to:

- need more time to learn
- need more time to think
- need more time to practice
- need more time with a teacher

To help parents in their efforts to accept their child, I ask them to put themselves in their child's shoes. Mom and Dad need to pretend what it's like to be their child and imagine what his life is like in the family. Imagine feeling that you are letting your parents down. Imagine feeling that you are a disappointment to your parents. Imagine feeling that you cannot please or impress the two most important people in the whole world for you. This technique of imagining themselves as their child helps parents experience and feel their child's pain and shame.

Next, parents must become aware of how the child's poor performance in school has changed his relationship with them. Problems in school almost always create problems at home. When parents are able to imagine fully what it's like to be their child, they should begin to feel more sympathy and compassion for their son. It is this sympathy and compassion that will help inspire them to see how important it is to accept the child's individuality. Each child is unique, and the goal for a parent is to respond to this uniqueness and to help each child to be all he can be in life. As you begin to accept your child more fully, look for what is special about him. Start focusing on what you love best about your child. When a child knows he is accepted, it provides a huge boost to his self-esteem, which is a major step toward helping slow learners find more happiness in life. It will also bring parents and their children closer together.

Always remember that the worst thing you can do to a slow learner is to try to transform that child into what he is not. I find that high-powered, high-achieving, perfection-driven parents often fall into this trap. These high-achieving parents just cannot accept that not every one of their children will be a success at learning. The tragedy for these parents is that they fail to appreciate their child's special qualities and, in the process, they drive their child into a pattern of failure at school and at home that often results in a lifetime of unhappiness and sometimes alienation.

2. Be Your Child's Advocate

Most parents generally are their child's advocate. This means they look out for their child's best interests and help others to understand the needs of their child. Good parents advocate for their children. It is especially important, however, for parents of a slow learner to advocate for the child because schools often overlook the needs of those who take a bit longer to catch on to the lesson. It is not that schools are prejudiced against slow learners; it's just that these educational institutions are busy places attempting to manage the learning process for many children. So it is easy for the needs of one child or a few children to be overlooked or for their needs to be misunderstood. Schools unknowingly label slow learners as children who are lazy or immature. A good time to advocate for your child is at the beginning of every new school year. It is especially important for parents to meet their child's new teacher each fall because most likely the new teacher will know very little about your child when school opens. When you meet your child's new teacher, be sure you share your child's special needs as a slow learner and also point out her strengths. Do your best to team up with the new teacher by letting her know that you will do all you can to work with her. I strongly recommend, whenever possible, that both parents should go to school to meet the new teacher. It has been my experience that teachers tend to be more responsive to the needs of a child when both parents participate in school conferences. When parents advocate for their child, they often see the learning environment in school improve because the teacher has become more sensitive to their child's needs. Parents comment to me they cannot believe how much happier their child is in school after a successful school visit.

The slow learner who feels accepted, both by her parents and by her teacher, will frequently be more motivated in school.

3. Schedule Yearly Evaluations

Since your child is a slow learner, you must protect him from falling behind academically. A child who has fallen behind by two or more grade levels is at serious risk for hating school. One of the best ways to protect your child from hating school is to check his academic status at the end of each year. In this way you will have his IQ and achievement scores to help plan placement for next year along with whatever extra help will be needed.

The best way to obtain a school checkup for your child, in my opinion, is to consult an experienced child psychologist, who may be recommended by your pediatrician. There are three advantages to obtaining a private evaluation outside of the school. First, you won't have to wait. In many schools today the school psychologist is assigned more children than he or she has time for. Consequently, the list of children who need to be evaluated can be quite long. Second, a private practitioner has far more time to dedicate to your child than an overscheduled school psychologist. And third, a private practitioner is often in a better position professionally to assess how your child is doing emotionally. Is your child's self-esteem okay? Does he feel confident? Is he feeling good about his friendships? Does he feel he is an important part of the family? Are there any emotional factors affecting his level of achievement? These are all important questions to be answered in addition to looking at your child's intellectual functioning and academic progress. Yearly checkups are a must when your child is a slow learner. It is the best way for parents to become aware of any problems that require their immediate attention.

4. Rely on Tutors

The best way for a child to learn is to have her very own teacher. Since this is not financially practical in our public school system, we give one teacher an entire classroom of children to teach. In many private schools children benefit from sharing their teacher with only twelve to fifteen fellow students. In public schools, children must share their teacher with upward of twenty-five or thirty other children. Studies have shown time and again that the smaller the class, the better children will learn. Nevertheless, we often overlook what a powerful tool individual tutoring can be for helping a child to learn. Private tutoring helps children to catch up to their current grade level, and private tutoring helps the slow learner to cope with public school classes that are not designed to meet her special needs.

Once a child falls behind academically, it is very unlikely she will be able to catch up simply by attending class. She will need the special attention that tutoring can provide. Weekly private tutoring is also a great alternative to having a child repeat a grade. This is particularly important once a child progresses to the fourth grade level, which seems to be the point at which the humiliation of being held back a grade is most keenly felt.

I strongly believe that parents of a slow learner will need to rely on tutoring from time to time to help their child advance throughout the elementary and high school years.

Here is some helpful advice on choosing the right tutor for your child.

- Look for teachers who are drawn to the age of the children they teach. These are professionals who might find five-year-olds to be a special challenge because they show great creative potential. Perhaps the teacher gravitates toward seven-year-olds because she sees them as tremendously inquisitive. Enthusiasm in a tutor helps to inspire a child struggling with school.
- Look for teachers who know you cannot motivate children through fear. An intimidating teacher fosters anxiety in a child that can inhibit the learning process
- Look for teachers who know there are many sources of

knowledge besides schools and books, such as instructional videos, computer programs, and field trips.

- Look for teachers who have more than one way to teach a subject. You want a tutor who is versatile and creative in helping your child to grasp material that is difficult for her.

- Look for teachers who have a great personality. Paul Pulling, a great educator, defined teaching as, "the transmission of knowledge through personality." Teaching is an art, and a teacher's personality is crucial to successful teaching, especially with a slow learner. When parents find the right tutor, children tell me they look forward to their private lessons. They also are happier when faced with school work.

5. Help Your Child Find a Passion in Life

Chances are high that your slow learner will never experience a lot of satisfaction as a student. To help compensate for this experience, parents need to find interests and activities outside of school that the child has a talent for and can truly enjoy. These experiences work like magic to help children feel good about themselves, and they help make up for the discouraging feelings that come from school. I remember a nine-year-old boy who was a classic slow learner. He shocked his parents by showing an interest in the violin. I, too, was hesitant about advising violin lessons because this boy's penmanship was so poor it was difficult to make out his name when he wrote it. But I had learned over the years to always give kids the benefit of the doubt and give them the chance to try something out. Well, to our surprise this little guy loved the violin and excelled at it.

Another little boy I knew went out for the football team. His mother almost rejected his interested in football because of her fear that he would be injured. Despite her anxiety about her son being hurt, Mom said he could play. He was so good at it that his success on the football field helped take a lot of the sting out of his less-than-stellar academic performance.

When children find a passion in life, their confidence increases. They also learn the self-discipline they need to succeed at more academic tasks.

I wasn't a slow learner in school, but I sure had to work hard to keep my grades up. As a result, I didn't feel very good about myself. Fortunately, my parents owned a candy store and ice cream parlor. Each day after high school I was expected to show up and help out with the family business. It was my job to make all the ice cream and the syrups for the store. To everyone's surprise and mine, I was really good at this. I received much praise and recognition from customers and from my family. I can't tell you what this did for my self-esteem and self-confidence. So make a real effort to experiment with all sorts of interests and activities until you find one that really turns your slow learner on.

6. Avoid Summer School

This recommendation may shock you. It will especially bother some teachers. I base this recommendation on my experience with summer school programs. I have rarely seen slow learners profit enough from attending summer school programs to justify the negative effect these programs have on such children. Summer school not only robs the slow learner of a much-needed vacation from school, but it is often perceived as a punishment. The progress I have seen from summer school is so limited that I believe it is not worth the risk of upsetting the slow-learning child with an experience he most likely will hate. Instead of summer school, I recommend private one-on-one tutoring. A skilled teacher has at her disposal many different ways of teaching each subject. Once a tutor finds an approach that works, she can make real progress with your child. Also, a teacher who loves her profession can help children to enjoy learning. You can find tutors by word of mouth or by asking your school for a list of teachers who are available over the summer. You can also rely on tutoring centers that are franchised throughout the country. Many parents have been satisfied by relying on a commercial tutoring service.

When I was a third grader, I was tutored every Saturday morning in reading and arithmetic. I still can remember sitting at the kitchen table on Saturday while Mrs. Bolt patiently helped me to catch up. I truly remember feeling relieved that I was no longer behind in my studies, and I felt as though I was just as good as the other kids. Years later when I became a child psychologist I frequently recommended tutoring, and I have never regretted doing so. In fact, for many years I ran a tutoring service from my office. After the psychologists had left for the day, five handpicked teachers entered the office to work with children who were behind in school. Tutoring works!

7. Avoid Resource Room Assistance

This is another recommendation that will upset some schools. Resource Room assistance is actually tutoring right in the school. Sometimes it is offered on a one-on-one basis or with a very small group of children. The problem with Resource Room assistance is that a child is often taken out of a class to be tutored. So while he is getting help with reading, he is falling behind in math or missing some special activity like physical education or art, which he really enjoys. I never could quite understand this self-defeating approach to helping a child in school. Some schools now avoid taking a child out of class and try to schedule Resource Room assistance when the child is not going to miss something important. Under these circumstances, I would recommend taking advantage of the extra help that schools can provide. But do avoid Resource Room assistance if it means your child will be taken out of some other class.

8. Change Your Attitude about Mistakes

Most of us have been brought up to feel embarrassed and ashamed when we make a mistake. This is unfortunate because it is impossible to learn anything without making mistakes. Some of the best teachers I have had as an adult have made me make mistakes on purpose. When I was learning to ski, my instructor told me to lean back on my skis to see what would happen. Of course, when I did lean back, I immediately lost control of my skis and quickly learned from this mistake. While I was learning to fly an airplane, my flight instructor told me to land the plane on purpose at a speed higher than what is recommended. I followed his instructions and immediately the plane bounced back into the air when the tires hit the runway. This mistake quickly taught me how dangerous it is to ignore my airspeed when landing. I'm sure what I'm saying to you as a parent is a not an altogether new idea. Mistakes are unavoidable when we are in the process of learning new skills. Mistakes are actually helpful in teaching students the right way to do something. My own personal motto is: "Every time I make a mistake, I'm that much closer to getting it right."

Normally, teachers and parents overreact to mistakes. When I was a seventh grader, my teacher would shake me when I gave the wrong answer in class. Today she would probably be cited for child abuse, but years ago this was acceptable and by no means uncommon. The giant red check marks after every mistake you made on a school assignment were also standard procedure. Is it any wonder so many of us grew up fearful of making mistakes and feeling humiliated when we got something wrong? To help your slow learner you are going to need a whole new attitude about mistakes. And that attitude is:

ADULTS AND CHILDREN CANNOT LEARN WITHOUT MAKING MISTAKES. MISTAKES ARE OPPORTUNITIES FOR PARENTS TO SHOW THEIR CHILDREN A BETTER WAY.

When parents take this approach with their slow learner, they are amazed to see how their child stops being fearful and defensive and approaches academic tasks with renewed enthusiasm.

9. Find the Right School for Your Child

Not every parent has the means to pay for a private school. But this is an option if you can afford the extra expense. I have known many parents who have been able to find a private or parochial school where the classes were small and the teachers were extra supportive. Some private schools actually cater to children who find school especially difficult. One of the advantages of this kind of school is that in it a child can feel like he fits in and he feels comfortable knowing that his classmates are similarly situated.

SUMMARY

The secret to succeeding with slow learners is to intervene early in the lives of these children while they are still in the elementary years. The recommendations in this chapter and the suggested readings can go a long way toward helping you succeed in making your slow learner a happier child.

Many of the children I have treated over the years are now parents themselves, so I can speak with some authority that I have seen many slow-learning children grow up to live very productive and happy lives.

RESOURCES

If you would like to learn more about how to help your slow learner, I suggest the following books and tutoring Web site:

A Mind at a Time, by Melvin Levine (New York: Simon & Schuster, 2002).

The Pressured Child: Helping Your Child Find Success in School and Life, by Michael Thompson, PhD, with Teresa Barker (New York: Ballantine, 2004).

Quirky Kids: Understanding and Helping Your Child Who Doesn't Fit In—When to Worry and When Not to Worry, by Perri Klass, MD, and Eileen Costello, MD (New York: Ballantine, 2003).

The Slow Learner in the Classroom, by Newell Carlyle Kephart (Columbus, OH: Merrill, 1971).

Teaching Students with Learning Problems, 5th ed., by Cecil D. Mercer and Ann R. Mercer (New York: Prentice-Hall, 1998).

When You Worry about the Child You Love: Emotional and Learning Problems in Children, by Edward M. Hallowell (New York: Simon & Schuster, 1996).

http://www.Educate.com, the Sylvan Learning Center.

CHAPTER 4

PEER REJECTION, PEER CRUELTY

INTRODUCTION

*C*hildren need friends! Without friends, a child's emotional development will be impaired. Friendships are as basic to a child's emotional health as good nutrition is to a child's physical health.

The need for children to be with others their own age surfaces early. We know that even babies seek out other children they see in a room. By age three, children are enthusiastically talking about their friends. By kindergarten, the average child has developed about five friendships.

THE PROBLEM

The absence of friendships in the life of a child is a major cause of unhappiness. A child without friends will not only be unhappy, but will very likely be at risk for becoming immature and for developing emotional problems.

It has been my experience that many parents are not aware of how important friends are to a child. In fact, many parents minimize the seriousness of their child being without friends by concluding that their child is going through some stage or phase. I can understand this reaction because it is certainly normal for children to have peer problems from time to time. But a child who is consistently rejected by other children is in a highly stressful situation that cannot be considered normal. Some children who are consistently rejected will express their unhappiness by withdrawing and spending hours in solitary, isolated play. Some will express their unhappiness by becoming aggressive toward other children. And still others will express their unhappiness by taking on a posture of arrogance and acting superior to any other children. Unfortunately, the rejected child who responds by becoming isolated or aggressive or arrogant only makes life worse for himself.

Children who are rejected usually are left alone and ignored by their peers. But some rejected children are not left alone; they, in addition, experience considerable cruelty from other kids. Peer cruelty in our schools is now at an all-time high. It is estimated that over 160,000 children are afraid to go to school each day. They are afraid of being abused by their classmates. It is a nightmare for a child to be so victimized. In our high-tech world, children are even being abused by other kids using instant messaging on the Internet. Some children are so negatively affected that they have been driven to take their lives in order to escape the pain, hurt, and abuse they endure at the hands of others. And a few children have been pushed so far that they have become school shooters, taking revenge on their tormentors. Listen to what some children have to say about being rejected or being treated cruelly by peers.

THE CHILDREN SPEAK

Bill is a nine-year-old fourth grader whose parents had to transfer him to another school because the bullying and abuse in his previous school was so out of control. Listen to what Bill had to say about his experience:

"It was awful. Every day was hell. I hated going to school. The name-calling was endless. I was called Dumbo ears, giraffe neck, faggot, queer, retard, injun, slope head, ass, bastard, loser, stupid, and coward. The teachers just ignored what the mean kids in school were doing. They didn't seem to care."

Jim, a ten-year-old fifth grader who is legally blind, described his experience:

"Kids hid my clothes during gym so I would be late for class and then laughed at me because the teachers scolded me for being late. I never had a good year in school. They were all terrible. I felt like I was nothing."

Lisa, a ten-year-old fifth grader, used to beg her mother to stay home. This is how Lisa described a typical school day:

> "They waited for me to get off the school bus and they would spit at me and make fun of me. They teased me because I didn't have a father and they knocked my things off my desk. The girls had a contest to see who could come up with the best name to call me. I wanted to die to get away from them.
>
> "At first I had a lot of friends, but as the bullying got worse, my friends began to cheer the bullies on. There wasn't a day when they didn't trip me or take my stuff or smash my lunch or make fun of me. They threatened to kill my dog. I kept thinking to myself, 'What is wrong with me? Why do they hate me?'"

Eleven-year-old Max had to be home schooled to escape his tormentors:

> "I'm tired of not being respected. Nobody likes me but the teachers. I feel like they are torturing me. It is so bad I'm always thinking about violence to get back at them. I'm so angry I'm thinking of taking a ten-inch knife to school. They all make me feel like an idiot. I hate them all."

Only in the last few years has peer rejection, peer cruelty, and bullying been taken seriously by parents, teachers, and school administrators. In the past, this kind of behavior was considered typical of children and, for the most part, harmless. Recent studies, however, clearly show that peer cruelty psychologically damages a child's personality. The daily barrage of insults, name-calling, and humiliating experiences results in a child hating herself. *The child who is abused eventually comes to believe what her tormentors are saying.* She becomes brainwashed by them and eventually concludes that she is in fact worthless. This damage to a child's personality can last a lifetime. In addition to self-hate, the abused child very often develops an inner rage resulting from being so mistreated. This inner rage can result in depression and in extreme situations in suicide and acts of revenge.

Unfortunately, parents are often in the dark when it comes to peer rejection and bullying, because the bullied child keeps secret his misery at school and the rejected child gives the appearance of merely going through a normal childhood phase. Consequently, parents, who are in the best position to help their child, often do not know the child is suffering and is in need of help. In the early stages of peer rejection and cruelty, the child feels unhappy, but within months this unhappiness can quickly turn into self-loathing and depression.

SOLUTIONS

1. Parents need to place the monitoring of their child's social life at the top of their list of priorities. Just as

they monitor their child's physical health, parents must also monitor their child's social interactions. You'll want to observe your son or daughter in the neighborhood to see how successfully friends are made and kept. And you'll want to collect various observations from teachers and others at the school regarding your child's social life. Always make it a point to ask your child's teacher the following questions:

- How is my child doing socially?
- Does she have friends?
- Does she have a best friend?
- Is my child a desired playmate?
- Do other children seek her out to play?
- Is my child able to make and keep friends?

Ask these questions of your child's teacher on a regular basis. Peer relationship problems are as serious as a child running a fever and should not be ignored.

2. I strongly recommend that whenever you have any suspicion that your child is being rejected or bullied, you should take on the role of a detective and explore in every way possible what is going on in your child's life outside of the home. Here are some behaviors to look for that can indicate that your child is being rejected by peers or being treated cruelly or bullied in school:

- being moody, irritable
- having little sense of humor and rarely smiling
- frequently playing alone and staying in the house
- receiving few, if any, phone calls from peers who want to play
- never or hardly ever receiving invitations to attend birthday parties or other special events
- reluctance to leave home and attend school
- complaints of feeling too ill to go to school
- declining grades
- crying easily and frequently
- statements describing himself as stupid and/or ugly
- statements of "I hate my life" and "I wish I was dead"
- withdrawing from the family
- appearing preoccupied and distant
- being temperamental
- having a low tolerance for frustration
- avoiding going out into the neighborhood

3. If you conclude that your child is friendless but not being abused by other children, then set the goal of helping your child establish at least one solid friendship. One good friend can go a long way toward helping a rejected child start developing social confidence. With this goal in mind, start observing your child with other children. As you observe, ask yourself this question: "How does my child's behavior discourage children from being his friend?" You must figure out why your child is not valued as a friend if

you are going to help him. The following list of questions will assist you to analyze why your child is poor at developing friendships.

- Does my child lack manners?
- Is my child a boring playmate with limited interests?
- Is my child a poor sport and temperamental when things don't go his way?
- Does my child break rules when playing games?
- Is my child overly aggressive?
- Does my child always have to have her way?
- Does my child call names and insult children when upset?
- Is my child so shy he withdraws from most social situations?
- Does she laugh and make fun of other children?
- Does he tease other children?
- Is she overly silly?
- Does he act arrogant and bossy?
- Does she always have to be first?
- Is he ever apologetic?
- Is she unkind and mean on purpose?
- Does he take toys without asking?
- Does she jump from one activity to another without first finishing what she started?
- Does he laugh at and ridicule other children?

This is not a comprehensive list, but it will give you some idea of how to look for the reasons underlying a child's lack of popularity. As you proceed to explore the reasons further, I suggest you ask relatives and teachers and siblings for their thoughts. Once you have an understanding of how your child spoils his friendships, you are in a position to start helping him to become more socially successful.

You start by becoming your child's advocate. After praising your child for the things he does well, point out that there is one area where he is having a hard time. You see, it is always easier for a child to look at his faults after he has heard compliments about what he does well. Ask your child if he knows what specific problem is giving him a hard time. If he seems confused as to what you are talking about, just say, "I think you would like very much to have more friends and I want to show you how to do better at making and keeping friends." As a parent you can certainly use your own words. I'm just giving you an example of how you might approach this problem. By taking your child's side to help him with a problem, you become his advocate. As an advocate you have a better chance of gaining his cooperation.

Next, invite your son to tell you how good friends behave. You can help your child if he gets stuck at times. For example, you can say, "Well, a good friend is kind and doesn't call you names or hurt your feelings." Then ask what else do you want in a good friend? Little by little you will establish a list of behaviors that characterize a good friend. For instance, good friends don't make fun of you or break your toys or are bossy or refuse to share. Then make another list of behaviors. This list will be made up of behaviors that make kids say, "Yuk . . . I don't want him to be my friend." Someone who lies or steals or makes fun of you or won't help you is not being a good friend. After the second list is complete, you then ask your child to look over the first list and ask him if he can see any behaviors he does that might bother a friend. The goal here is to begin to make your child aware of how he behaves with others. Only when a child discovers how he himself handles other children poorly can he really change. Listen to how a ten-year-old boy expressed himself after he gained awareness of how he was spoiling his friendships.

> "I need to be kinder, less sarcastic, and not draw attention to myself by doing stupid stuff. I need to be less cynical and not put people down, stop doing annoying things, and stop talking so much."

When a rejected child finally attains this kind of insight into himself, he will stop blaming others for being so unpopular and begin to behave differently to attract friends.

Let's review: It's important for parents to monitor their child's social life. If there are problems, then the parent must take on the role of a detective and find out what is going on. Is your child being rejected by peers? If she is being rejected, you need to discover why other children do not value your child as a friend. Once you have this answer, you can begin to coach your child by making her aware of the ways she performs well in social settings and what behaviors of a negative type need work if she is to improve her relationships with others. Here are some additional tips for helping your rejected child to succeed in developing friendships.

4. Arrange some playtime at your home, but keep the number of children down to no more than two. At first, I would recommend just one child coming over to play. Your child will have a better chance of succeeding with one child at a time, and you will have an easier time observing how the children interact with each other. After the play session, review with your child in what ways he was a good friend and gently advise him where he needs to make some changes. Sometimes it is necessary for a parent to intervene while the children are playing because the situation is going poorly. At these times call your child into another room, so you don't embarrass him, and coach him to stop whatever he is doing that encourages a negative response from his playmate. Structured playtimes like this can help a rejected child gain confidence by forming one solid friendship from which others can be built.

5. Social skills have to be learned just like a child learns to read. This means of course that your child will need to practice these skills in order to become more

adept at cultivating friends. Therefore, it is very helpful to enroll a child having problems with peers in some sort of club or organization. Consider Boy Scouts, Girl Scouts, team sports, the YMCA, or the YWCA. The Boys & Girls Club is another idea. Look around for clubs in and out of school that your child can join and get practice at being a good friend.

6. I also suggest you make your child's teacher aware of your concerns. A teacher is in a very good position to facilitate friendships in her class and to give a youngster tips on how to be a better friend and to point out when he is (and is not) being a good friend.

7. During the summer, look for day camps or overnight camps where your child can learn new skills and also have a chance to make friends. As a child learns new skills, she becomes a more confident and more interesting potential friend. I also suggest that you inform the camp director about your child's need for some help with making and keeping friends so the director can be aware of opportunities to help your child with his social skills.

8. Make sure your child is learning good manners at home. Children who greet others courteously, say thank you, know how to apologize, and do favors for others are socially attractive to others. I have always noticed in my practice that children without friends generally have poor manners.

9. Help your child build up confidence by teaching him new games to play and helping him to develop skills like roller-blading, bike riding, ice skating, skiing, golf, bowling, and so on. Every child needs to feel especially good at one or more activities or interests so his confidence will grow.

10. Some schools offer group peer counseling to help kids with their social skills. If your school offers this kind of program, consider enrolling your child.

11. It might be useful to hire a male teenager for your son or a female teenager for your daughter, depending on who is having the problem, to spend time as a "baby sitter/companion" with your child while you are busy. Give the teen your permission to pass on some tips to your child regarding getting along with kids whenever it seems appropriate. Children will often be more open to receiving tips from a teen they look up to than from a parent. Choose a teen you know who is mature, responsible, and well liked.

12. Be on the lookout for those times when your child is especially compassionate or sensitive or helpful to others and bring this to his attention. This strategy is called "Catching Them When They Are Good." You are essentially rewarding the behavior you want to see develop in your child when he spontaneously produces it. For example, you might say something like,

"I was so impressed with the way you helped your friend out with his homework. That was really very nice."

What to Do If Your Child Is Being Bullied and Treated Cruelly by Peers

1. The first step is to stop the bullying. This means you will need to make the school aware of the problem. Many states today have legally required antibullying policies in place. The problem is that the "kids will be kids mentality" remains ingrained in our public school system. Therefore, parents will find that schools vary in how cooperative they are in helping to deal with this kind of problem. Some schools are behind the times, and the principal may tell you that unless school officials see the problem they cannot do anything about it. Other schools are on top of this problem, and the principal will tell you she will alert the entire staff including the bus driver and cafeteria monitors to find out what is going on. Obviously the latter school will be easier to work with, but you must hang in there and insist on the school's help. I have found that schools generally respond better when both parents take the time to come in and talk with the principal or the teacher or the school counselor.

   Schools have several options for dealing with peer cruelty. They can bring the children together and help them mediate better ways of getting along or talk with the child(ren) doing the bullying and inform them that their behavior must stop and that there will be consequences such as:

- contacting the parents of the bully
- suspending the bully (or bullies)
- arranging a meeting between all the parents whose children are involved to elicit everyone's cooperation to solve the problem

Sometimes bullying and peer cruelty are so severe that parents need to consider consulting a lawyer to file charges with the police. Sometimes the situation is so hopeless that parents need to consider transferring their child to another school. The bottom line is: parents must intervene when they discover their child is being abused and harassed.

2. When bullying occurs, it is good advice to tell your child to do her best to avoid the kids who are bullying and to stay close to friends.

3. It is also good advice to tell your child to avoid going into areas alone, especially those that are unsupervised or not supervised very well at school, such as stairwells, the playground, and the cafeteria.

4. Encourage your child to continue making friends. The tips in this chapter can help you to help your child to be more popular.

5. Some children who are bullied have gotten into some self-defeating patterns of behavior with peers. As a result, they at times unwittingly invite peers to attack them by lying, bragging, and acting inappropriately in class. If this is the case with your child, you might consider counseling sessions with a child psychologist. One-on-one counseling sessions can be very helpful in teaching a child victimized by bullies a better way to handle himself in stressful situations.

SUMMARY

One of the major sources of unhappiness in children is rejection by their peers. In this chapter, I have presented some of the best strategies I know for parents to help their child to become more popular. It has been my experience that unhappy children dramatically improve as they learn how to make and keep friends.

RESOURCES

If you would like to learn more, I recommend the following books:

Best Friends, Worst Enemies, by Michael Thompson, PhD, and Catherine O'Neill Grace, with Lawrence J. Cohen, PhD (New York: Ballantine, 2001).
Bullies and Victims: Helping Your Child through the Schoolyard

Battlefield, by SuEllen Fried and Paula Fried, PhD (New York: M. Evans & Company, 1996).

Bullies: Targets and Witnesses Helping Children Break the Pain Chain, by SuEllen Fried and Paula Fried, PhD (New York: M. Evans & Company, 2003).

The Hidden Gifts of the Introverted Child: Helping Your Child Thrive in an Extroverted World, by Marti Olsen Laney, PsyD (New York: Workman, 2005).

Mom, They're Teasing Me: Helping Your Child to Solve Social Problems, by Michael Thompson, Lawrence L. Cohen, and Catherine O'Neill Grace (New York: Ballantine, 2004).

Queen Bees & Wannabes: Helping Your Daughter Survive Cliques, Gossip, Boyfriends & Other Realities of Adolescence, by Rosalind Wiseman (New York: Three Rivers Press, 2002).

The Shyness Breakthrough: A No-Stress Plan to Help Your Shy Child Warm Up, Open Up, and Join the Fun, by Bernardo J. Carducci, PhD (New York: St. Martin's, 2003).

CHAPTER 5

QUARRELING PARENTS

INTRODUCTION

When adults marry or choose to live together as a couple, they soon discover that along with their similarities, they have differences as well. Attitudes toward managing money, expectations regarding sex, problems with in-laws or extended family members, and differences in religious beliefs are just some of the areas where conflicts can arise. This is a normal part of sharing one's life with someone. Differences, however, can increase dramatically with the birth of a child. In the first year after the birth of a baby, couples face many new responsibilities, along with the challenge of learning to share this new role as parent. Couples also find that their more carefree lifestyle and spontaneous love life change with the birth of their baby. Newborns complicate the relationship between two adults, and the opportunities to disagree and quarrel increase dramatically.

There are many ways to deal with differences in a relationship, and each couple has its own unique obstacles to overcome.

Some couples are more adept than others at dealing with these challenges. Many new moms and dads rise to the occasion and find ways to constructively overcome their differences. Others sink into constant bickering and lash out at each other. A few couples actually experience violence in their relationship.

THE PROBLEM

If someone were to take a survey and ask parents the question "Should parents fight in front of their children?" the vast majority of couples would say no. Parents instinctively know the right way to behave in front of their children. However, most parents, once they become angry and upset, set good sense aside, ignore their better judgment, allow personal emotions to run rampant, and vent their hostilities even if the children happen to be in the room or within earshot.

Today, a large body of research clearly shows that children whose parents continually bicker and fight in their presence are incredibly unhappy, and this state of mind can damage them for life. Parents need to be aware that their fighting can be harmful to the children. When confronted with this reality, all too many parents attempt to minimize how much their fighting affects their children.

Child psychologists and mental health professionals who treat children know from experience that children who are routinely exposed to parental fighting:

- become terribly frightened because to children their parents are their whole world and their major source of security. If their parents appear to be out of control, they lose their sense of security.

- will find their feelings of fear turning into anxiety. Anxiety is an emotional state characterized by intense apprehension coupled with feelings of impending doom. The fear is a specific part of each instance of the parents doing battle with one another, but the feeling of anxiety spreads out to affect all aspects of a child's life.
- become hypervigilant; they are in a super alert state and on edge as they wait for something terrible to happen. These children become ever watchful for any clues suggesting that their parents are going to have another nasty fight.
- develop defense mechanisms to handle the unhappiness and anxiety they experience at home. There are five different responses children develop:

1. Some children will throw themselves into the middle of the fight to get their parents to stop. With this pattern the child actually tries to break up the fighting and act as a peacemaker. Sometimes, children are physically hurt this way.
2. Other children simply withdraw. They hide and plug up their ears. These children are retreaters. They retreat to a closet or their bedroom or turn the volume up on their iPod or pile pillows on top of their heads.
3. Sometimes children will take sides, deciding that one parent is the good parent and the other is the bad parent. With this pattern the child can eventually become alienated from a parent.

4. Then there are those children who will purposely misbehave. These children become aggressive in order to distract the parents from their own fighting by forcing the parents to discipline them.

5. Finally, there are the children who emotionally distance themselves from both parents. With this pattern these children mentally live apart from their parents. They no longer think of their parents as people they can trust or respect or to whom they would look for help.

Continued bouts of parental fighting, bickering, and quarreling at home can often result in the children exhibiting very negative behaviors toward others:

- Some children can take their anger for their parents out on teachers and become behavior problems in school.
- Other kids mistreat their brothers and sisters in ways that are nasty and cruel. Sibling rivalry often becomes intense in homes where the parents frequently quarrel, bicker, and fight. It has been my experience that the worst cases of sibling rivalry occur in families where the parents are out of control with their quarreling.

Continued fighting also can change the way a mother and a father parent their children. I have found that parents who exhibit a pattern of fighting become overly critical of their children's behavior because they are quite often angry. Angry parents tend to overreact to the annoying behaviors their children normally act out. Children can become like lighting rods, attracting their parent's anger simply by misbehaving when Mom or Dad is in an angry state. I have also found that moms and dads who fight excessively often alienate the child from the other parent. For example, the child may not want to have anything to do with his father because the mother incessantly badmouths the father. The parent actually discredits the other parent to such a degree that the child feels a loss of love toward that parent. Arguing or expressing heated differences of opinion from time to time is normal in most households. Such clashes are part of the family dynamic in most homes. But fighting in a way that is nasty and destructive to the relationship itself, however, is not normal. Children who live in homes in which such fighting takes place suffer emotionally. Their childhood becomes very unhappy, and as teens and adults they often have serious problems committing themselves to intimate relationships and continue the pattern of conflict.

If you have difficulty controlling your temper when arguing with your spouse or partner, you needn't despair. The fact that this chapter is pressing you to question your own behavior is an important first step toward making your life and the lives of your partner and your children better. I suggest you share this chapter with your spouse or partner and start working together for the welfare of your unhappy child.

THE CHILDREN SPEAK

While preparing this chapter, I had a conversation with a sixty-five-year-old gentleman. As I talked to him about the chapter on parents fighting, he volunteered the following story. I have included it because even at his age the child within him lives on and he still suffers with the memories of his parents' fights:

"My parents mostly fought at night. My father wouldn't come home from work until around 1:30 AM, so their fights were in the middle of the night. I had two younger sisters. We would be sound asleep and all of a sudden the screaming and the yelling would start. It was awful. We were all terrified. The next day, I remember going off to school wondering if my parents were going to get a divorce. I worried a lot about that. The fights would leave me feeling unhappy for days, and just about when I began to feel okay, they would have another one.

"I will never forget one night when my younger sister began to shake uncontrollably as my parents started up with another fight. Her mouth was chattering and her body was trembling. I never saw anything like that before. I thought she was going to die. When my parents saw her, they stopped fighting for a minute, and then they started up again as my mother blamed my father for my sister's condition. My father left the room as my mother tried to calm my sister down. And then it happened. My mother told me to go upstairs and give my father the empty suitcase she just handed me. 'Here,' she said, 'give this to your father and tell him to leave.' Would you believe I did just that? I was too scared not to obey. What an awful experience to hand your father a suitcase and tell him to leave. That night happened fifty-five years ago, and I can still see it in my head. I still feel so sad and sick when that scene flashes through my mind. In fact, right now I feel like crying after telling you this story. All that fighting really changed my sister's personality. She can't deal with any stress. Now any time something unpleasant happens, she puts on a smile and changes the subject. She is like the proverbial ostrich that sticks its head in the sand. I hope your book helps parents to realize that their fighting makes kids unbelievably unhappy and can leave them with some awful memories that never go away."

This story reminded me of a young college student who came to see me on one of her breaks. She was a bright, attractive young woman but so sad. I will call her Mary for the sake of confidentiality. Mary told me she couldn't wait to go away to college to escape her parents' constant bickering and fighting. As long as she could remember they fought, and the fights occurred several times a week. I will never forget the pain Mary experienced living with two parents she loved who had no love for each other. Mary came to see me because, even though she was away at college, she could not escape her parents' fights. She heard about the fights when she called home and she witnessed the fights again when both parents came to visit her at college. Mary explained to me,

"I get so stressed out when they both come to visit me. It's like I'm walking on eggs, afraid that something I say will start a fight. It's terrible to miss your parents and then when they come to visit, you can't wait for them to go. I finally got the courage to ask my parents to come one at a time and not together. I just can't take it anymore."

At the time of my first meeting with Mary, Christmas was just a few weeks away. Mary knew what Christmas was like at her home and she dreaded it. I diagnosed her as having Dys-thymia, a low-grade depression. People who have Dysthymia experience a continuous, steady, chronic, down feeling that remains with them every day. And it was this daily sadness that interfered with Mary's ability to concentrate at college and to have the energy to study. This young woman was president of an honor society and president of her sorority and had many friends. Nevertheless, the constant fighting by her parents put a cloud over her whole life and took the joy out of her accomplishments.

———

Recently, a mother brought her four-year-old daughter, Chelsea, to see me. According to the mother, Chelsea cried a lot, had a hard time falling asleep, often had nightmares, and was distant from her father. I met with this little girl in my office. She was the kind of child you want to take home. She was so cute and quite verbal for her age. After some cookies and milk, I asked her why she cried so much. This is what she said:

"They fighted again last night." I asked her who "fighted" and she answered, "My mom and my dad.

They fighted all the time." I asked her if their fighting was getting better or worse. Chelsea answered, "It's worser." And then she said, "They say bad words. They say the *F* word. I hate Dada because he be mean to Mama. . . . I don't love my dada any more." I asked her why she did not love her father anymore. Chelsea said, "'Cause he's mean to Mommy. He makes Mommy cry and I see him push her on purpose." And then Chelsea said, "I know my dada doesn't love my mama."

———

Another little four-year-old girl said this about her fighting parents: "Mommy and Daddy were fighting and Daddy threw Mommy's clothes in the driveway in garbage bags. Daddy is a mean daddy. He makes me sad."

———

Here are the comments of a fifteen-year-old boy when asked about his parents' constant quarreling. "They are like George Costanza's parents on *Seinfeld*. They fight over everything from the moment they get up to the time they get ready to go to bed. They are freakin' me out. I can't wait to go to college."

———

Up to this point, I have been focusing on parents who live together. But we now know that divorced parents who continue to fight can visit just as much grief on their children as the parents who live together. Over the past fifteen years, there has been considerable research done on the impact of parents fighting and quarreling during and after the divorce process. The findings are significant and impressive. They show that one of the major reasons for children becoming emotionally disturbed over their parents' divorce is the continued fighting that takes place after the divorce. I have seen many, many children who are in the unfortunate situation of having parents who never stopped the war. I have seen the fighting go on for as long as a decade or more after the divorce. These children have seen their parents key each other's cars, call the police on each other, and rant and rave in public. If ever you want to see some sad children, talk with youngsters who love their parents and are reminded almost daily that the parents they love, hate each other. The seemingly inexhaustible rage between parents causes their children immense suffering and sadness year after year. It is no different than what kids experience with quarreling parents who are living together.

SOLUTIONS

How can you tell if you and your spouse or partner are fighting too much in front of your children? Just ask yourself two questions:

- How many arguments do we have in a week? If you are not sure, take the time to count them over the next seven days.

- When we fight, do we engage in the following behaviors? Do we:

  yell and scream?
  swear and insult each other?
  throw and break things?
  withdraw into silence for hours or days?
  hit, shove, and push?

Your answers to these two questions will help you to determine whether or not the fighting in your home is excessive or out of control. You might also ask your children. Here is how you could pose the question.

"You know how kids fight and argue in school. Well, kids are not the only ones who fight and argue. Grown-ups argue and fight, too. I want to ask you a question and I want you to be real honest. Don't be afraid to answer. It won't make me mad. Do you think Dad and I argue a lot?"

What I'm asking you to do will take real courage. I'm urging you to examine your own behavior and that of your spouse or partner by asking yourselves very specific questions and by seeking out and carefully listening to the opinions of your children. This isn't easy, but the potential benefits to you and your family will be significant. If fighting is out of control in your house, you most likely have discovered why your children are so unhappy.

If you have decided that you and your spouse argue too

much and too often in front of the children, then you need to go on to the next step to bring about real, positive change in your family. The next step involves discovering the major reasons for your fights, quarrels, and bickering. You need to understand why it is so easy to drift into such behavior. In my opinion, the major sources of conflict between parents result from the following sources.

Mom Knows Best

A number of moms believe that many women know best when it comes to parenting the children and running the household. This belief, one that many women hold, is further supported by a good number of men. I suspect that many men grew up with this belief because that is what their own mothers communicated to them. This belief that Mom knows best contributes to so many problems in a marriage. A woman who takes this position may be overly critical of her husband for parenting or managing household matters differently than she would. In her mind, hers is the only way and the best way. This criticism often results in Dad taking a back seat in the parenting arena, leaving it mostly in Mom's hands. Mom, of course, feels this extra burden of having to do everything without the help of her husband, and so she becomes angry with him.

Listen to some of the comments mothers consistently make about their husbands:

> "My husband doesn't contribute at all. It's like having another child in the house."

"When my husband does help out, it's wrong and not worth the trouble to get him to chip in."

And from the fathers I hear:

"It always has to be her way. Nothing I do is ever right."

"She wants me to be her partner, but she has to be in charge of all the decisions. It always has to be her way."

Dad as "Mom's Helper"

Another source of friction between married couples focuses on comparing the nature of their relationship before children arrived to what it's like now that youngsters have entered the family. Before the kids come along, the husband is viewed as an equal partner with his wife. Once the children come, Dad is reduced in status to Mom's helper. Men hate being Mom's helper. For example, when Dad is gone and Mom is home, she is in charge of the kids. She is "MOM." When Mom is gone and Dad is home, Dad is "babysitting." When a man becomes Mom's helper, he waits to be told what to do with the children instead of digging in and taking the initiative.

Men Co-Parent and Co-Manage the Household When Their Schedules Permit

A further important source of discontent and resentment between parental partners is the continued reluctance of men to co-parent and co-manage the household. Despite the fact that men are doing far more today than their fathers did in physically caring for their children and spending time with them, 75 percent of dads are still not actively involved in daily care of the children or in sharing the household responsibilities. It has been my experience that if men help, they do so as their schedules permits.

When couples are raising a family, the three major sources of conflict I have just outlined account for the vast majority of the arguments, quarrels, and bickering that goes on in the marriage. The frustration, anger, and resentment that enter a marriage from these three sources can fuel enough discontent to last a lifetime. All too often those who suffer most are the children.

A Case in Point

Some time ago, a mother named Liz came to see me in my office. She was totally exasperated with her husband. "He doesn't do anything with the kids," she complained. "My children come to me for everything. I have four children and they are like my shadows. I can't even go to the bathroom without one of them calling out for something."

After listening to how unbearable things had become for her, I realized that as long as she was in the home, the children would never choose to seek out their father for anything. I brought this to her attention and encouraged her to try an experiment. She was to choose a time during the following week and leave the home. She was to go shopping, to a movie or some special event, or to visit a friend, but she was to go somewhere so her husband could be alone with the children on his own. I could tell that this mom was not very thrilled with my recommendation. She mumbled something about coming home to find the house a wreck and the kids running wild.

Despite her cynicism, she agreed to follow my advice. A week later she returned. When I met her in the waiting room, she had an annoyed look on her face. As she entered my office she said, "Well I did what you recommended and you won't believe what he did." I took a deep breath and asked her to tell me. "I came home," she said, with a very critical tone of voice, "and all the children were in their beds asleep wearing their summer pajamas."

"What is so terrible about this?" I asked.

She raised her voice and in the most annoyed way said, "It's winter outside and the children were in summer pajamas. We have enough bills without going to the pediatrician if they catch colds."

At this point I changed the subject and asked her what the children had to say about the evening with their father. "Oh," she said, "they loved it. They had so much fun they are still talking about it and want to know when they can stay home with Dad again."

I looked at this woman, who had not quite realized what she just said, and asked, "Isn't that what you wanted? Didn't you want your children more involved with their dad, and your husband doing more with the children?"

She looked stunned. I could see the light going off in her head. This mom, like so many moms, had fallen into the "Mom knows best" trap, which had pushed her husband into the background of their family life. She left my office determined to change her attitude and to appreciate that her husband may do things different from her, but that doesn't necessarily make him wrong.

At this point it should be obvious that arguing in front of the children causes them to become unhappy and can result in all sorts of personal and family problems. Becoming aware of the three main sources that provoke mothers and fathers to fight is crucial if you are to change your family life for the better. But this is only half the battle in reclaiming a happier home life. You must commit to take actions that will bring about the desired result. The following recommendations can help you significantly reduce the fighting in your home.

Recommendations for a More Peaceful Homelife

Here are some ideas that have helped other parents. I hope they will help you to overcome the quarreling and fighting in your home.

- For the men, start today to make the workload at home fairer. As long as your wife feels you have abandoned her and that she must run everything for the family, she will be filled with resentment. Ask your partner to list everything she does for the family and agree to also make your own list. Then meet in a few days somewhere away from the children to review your lists and to work out how to share more fairly the workload of having a family. When parents share giving the children baths, helping them with homework, and straightening up the house, a calmness comes over the family that is welcomed by everyone. *There is no better way for a man to lose his wife emotionally than to make her feel he has abandoned her as a husband and as a father.*

- For the women, make a promise, starting today, not to use yourself as the standard for how everything should be done in the family. Men and women see things differently and react differently. It is important for a mother to accept this and to appreciate that there is more than one way to do things, not just her way. *There is no better way for a woman to isolate herself from her husband than to convey to him that she knows best and must make all the important decisions with respect to managing the household and the children.*

- Work out an agreement with your spouse/partner to signal each other when you each sense your tempers are rising. The idea is to stop before you lose control in front of the children. Your goal is to postpone the argument till the children are not around.

- Make an effort to tone down the level of intensity of your arguments. In other words, have an agreement with your spouse/partner that, when an argument or quarrel surfaces, there will be no swearing, no name calling, and no insults.

- Schedule time outside the home in a public place such as a restaurant or a coffee house to discuss some of the differences that ignite arguments in the marriage. People tend to show more self-control and act more civil in a public setting.

- If you and your spouse/partner have a religious affiliation, consider receiving some pastoral counseling regarding the issues that keep surfacing in your marriage or relationship. Some couples are more open to seeing a priest or a pastor rather than a mental health professional.

- Be available to your children after they witness a fight between you and your spouse/partner. When children see their parents fight, they are left alone to conjure up all sorts of fears and worries. All too often, the parents themselves are too upset to think about their children's well-being. Make a real effort to comfort your children and to calm them down after they witness their parents fighting.

- When possible, let your children witness you and your spouse/partner making up. In research experiments, children who watched their parents make up immediately relaxed and became free from their distress. Hugs, kisses, and smiles are a great way to show children that Mom and Dad have made up. It also shows that their parents can have serious disagreements and still deeply love one another.

- If you feel the communication is so poor between you and your spouse/partner that these strategies aren't likely to work, then both of you should consider seeing a counselor. Many quarreling couples have been helped by a few sessions with a marriage or family counselor. I suggest you meet with a counselor even if your partner or spouse will not go to the first meeting. In my practice, I often meet with a husband or a wife and then find ways to bring the absent spouse into the process. I find that parents are motivated to go out of their way—

to try every avenue available to them—if the welfare of their children is at stake. If your spouse/partner resists counseling, try making the following point:

> "If *we* are feeling miserable in our marriage, you can imagine how the children feel living with us. Our children deserve to live in a peaceful home with parents who can solve their differences constructively. We owe it to them and to ourselves not to let this situation go on. We are *all* hurting."

SUMMARY

Parental bickering, quarreling, arguing, and fighting not only makes children tremendously unhappy, but the emotional, psychological, and family disruption can have devastating long-term effects on youngsters. You owe it to yourselves and your children to do everything possible to stop destructive patterns from becoming a part of family life. The advice and recommendations in this chapter will help you to help your unhappy child and give you a good start toward creating the kind of home life you have always dreamed of having.

RESOURCES

If you would like to learn more about solving this problem, I recommend the following books.

Custody Chaos, Personal Peace: Sharing Custody with an Ex Who Is Driving You Crazy, by Jeffrey Wittman, PhD (New York: Berkley Publishing Group, 2001).

Men Are from Mars, Women Are from Venus: A Practical Guide for Improving Communications and Getting What You Want in Your Relationships, by John Gray (New York: HarperCollins, 1992).

The Proper Care and Feeding of Husbands, by Dr. Laura Schlessinger (New York: HarperCollins, 2004).

What Children Learn from Their Parents' Marriage: It May Be Your Marriage, but It's Your Child's Blueprint for Intimacy, by Judith P. Siegel, PhD, CSW (New York: HarperCollins, 2000).

When Anger Hurts Your Relationship: 10 Simple Solutions for Couples Who Fight, by Kim Paleg, PhD, and Matthew McKay, PhD (Oakland, CA: New Harbinger Publications, 2001).

Why Parents Disagree: How Women and Men Parent Differently and How We Can Work Together, by Dr. Ron Taffel with Roberta Israeloff (New York: William Morrow, 1994).

CHAPTER 6

PARENTAL FAVORITISM

INTRODUCTION

"Mommy, am I your favorite?" It is the rare child who has not asked this question. Every child wants to be his or her parents' favorite. And almost every parent struggles to be fair with each child. It is humanly impossible for a parent not to feel a special attraction to one child at times. If a child is very social and the parents are socially outgoing, that child may be favored at times. If the parents are laid back and relaxed people, they may respond less favorably to their high-energy, hyper child at times. Parents face many challenges when raising their children, but none more intense than to appreciate each child's uniqueness and to keep favoritism under control. It is okay to feel a special attraction to one child. It is not okay actually to favor one child over another.

THE PROBLEM

Every parent knows the story of Cinderella, whose stepsisters were given special treatment by their mother while she was made to serve all of them rather than being recognized as their equal. The problem is that while most parents can spot favoritism in other families, they can't seem to recognize it in their own. They just do not see how they have come to prefer one child over the other. It is human nature for a parent to feel attracted to one child more than another. A father's success in sports as a youngster may find him more drawn toward his athletic son. A mother who is very feminine may find herself drawn to the daughter who is more like her, rather than her tomboy daughter. However, it is a failing in parenting to actually favor one child over another. The less-favored boy or girl can truly become an unhappy child.

Children are born with a set of traits that make up their temperament. Sometimes one child in a family has an easygoing temperament and the other child has a difficult temperament. This is why children in the same family can be very different. Here is a short list of some of the traits with which children come into this world:

outgoing	or	shy
cheerful	or	gloomy
calm	or	high-strung
stable mood	or	moody
deliberate	or	impulsive
focused	or	distractible
cooperative	or	stubborn

goal focused	or	gives up easily
flexible	or	possesses strong preferences
low keyed	or	loud

Some parents will favor a child with a temperament that is either easier to deal with than the other children's or more like their own. I recall an easygoing, relaxed, low-keyed father, who was quite turned off by his little boy. His child was gifted intellectually, high-strung, loud, active, and with strong preferences. Another dad with a different personality would have loved a son like this. I also recall a mother who couldn't warm up to her eight-year-old daughter. This mother looked at me and said, "At birth she came out screaming and she hasn't shut up yet!"

Sometimes certain children are less favored because they are born into a family during a difficult time. The negative circumstances of the family crisis becomes associated with the birth of the baby. The last thing the parents may want in their life at such a critical time is a baby who is naturally demanding and very needy.

Sometimes a woman unexpectedly conceives and gives birth to a baby soon after having adopted a child. The excitement of having "her own child," after years of believing this would be impossible, biases her (and possibly the father) to favor the biological child. There are even times when a family will almost split into factions over a situation like this. For example, Dad may feel bad that his wife favors her biological child, so he compensates by paying more attention to the adopted child. As the years pass the family becomes polarized, with Mom and the biological child at odds with Dad and the adopted child.

Depending upon the particular dynamic of the family, a disabled or special-needs child can be either the less-favored child or the favored one. Some parents become overwhelmed with guilt and sadness for the ill child and so dedicate themselves to this youngster, thereby leaving their other children on the sidelines desperately seeking attention, approval, affection, and emotional support. And sometimes the burden and heavy daily responsibility of parenting a sick, disabled, or special-needs child result in that youngster being less favored, again out of guilt, shame, or some type of revulsion that one or both parents might feel at not having borne a healthy baby.

Parents who were less favored as children sometimes repeat this experience with their own children by favoring one son or daughter over another. It is not uncommon for an emotionally damaged parent to recreate in her own family the exact same experience that caused her so much suffering as a child. I recall a mother attending her own mother's wake, looking down into the casket, and saying, "You never loved me." This woman had two children in her own family: one she loved and favored while the other was pushed aside.

A child might be less favored because she reminds one parent of his spouse/partner who he absolutely dislikes. Divorced parents at times find themselves in this situation. A divorced father seeing his ex-wife in his daughter may treat this child differently from the other children. A divorced mother seeing her ex-husband in her son may reject her son. Sometimes parents openly express their biased feelings by saying things like: "You're just as lazy as your father" or "You're as impossible as your mother." This biased response by a father or mother is very painful for a child, because children are who they are, and they know one parent resents them for it.

A parent might also favor the child who more easily shows her love. Since we all want to be loved, it is easy to favor a child who is always responding to us with affection. The more openly loving child can elicit feelings of favoritism in a parent. In such a case it would seem possible that the parent and the child might not even know that this favoring relationship is taking place. The child might be quite oblivious to the affection since he is universally affectionate, and the parent would simply absorb the affection and respond favorably irrespective of whether others in the family were similarly attracted to the child.

These are the major reasons why parents will favor one child over another. A parent who favors a child is a parent who behaves like a prejudiced person. Once the parent becomes prejudiced, the less-favored child is almost always seen in a bad light and is often in a no-win situation. No matter what the child does, she is in trouble. The bias the parent feels against the child is so strong that negatives are read into whatever the child does. The consequences for the less-favored child can be devastating because of the negative treatment and stricter discipline this boy or girl experiences day after day. Imagine how you would feel if you could not feel safe, loved, wanted, and admired by your own parents?

The Consequences of Favoritism

- feeling inferior
- feeling unlovable

- self-loathing
- self-mutilation
- chronic depression
- developing a submissive personality
- developing a victim mentality
- taking revenge by living the life of the "black sheep"
- basic mistrust for intimate relationships
- alienation from the family
- predisposition to create the same trauma with future children

To feel unloved and unwanted is a devastating experience for a child. This is especially true when the child sees all the love she craves going to other children in the family. The young mind of a child is unable to reason that it's really Mom or Dad who has the problem. The young mind of a child can only conclude, "There is something terribly wrong with me." Some victims of favoritism will live a submissive life, cowering with inferiority, while other children will take revenge on their parents by ruining their lives. Their thinking is: " I will be everything you don't want me to be and that will show you!" Sometimes this behavior actually forces the parent to give attention to the less-favored child, even though it is negative attention. Favoritism is one of the most serious problems in today's families. It is a problem parents commonly overlook, and when they do recognize it, they underestimate the impact it can have on a child's life.

THE CHILDREN SPEAK

"It's kind of like she doesn't love me. She loves my brother and forgets about me," said a ten-year-old boy about his life as a less-favored child.

———

Here an eight-year-old girl voices concern that her sister is favored over her:

"They [her mom and sister] don't really like me that much. It makes me feel really sad."

———

The anger this nine-year-old boy has for his mother spills out of him:

"My mom's favorites are my two sisters. She spends more time with them. She cuddles on the couch with them. She hardly ever punishes them. When I ask her to play she's always *too busy*. If I do something wrong, I'm immediately punished, where my sisters get second and third chances and they never get punished as hard as I do. I hate my mother. I don't think she loves me at all."

———

"I know I was my mom's favorite child, because she told me," a sixteen-year-old girl recalls. "She tried hard not to show it, but I knew how she felt. It was a terrible secret to keep, and I felt awful for my sisters. I will never ever do that to any of my children."

———

"I always knew my father wished I was a boy," one twelve-year-old girl told me while we were discussing why she believed her father favored her brother. "The only time he paid any attention to me was when I did something boyish. When my brother was born, I was seven. From that point on it was like I didn't exist. My father did everything with my brother. I can't remember the last time he said something nice to me or did something nice for me. I can't wait to grow up and get away from him."

———

These childhood feelings can extend well into adulthood. One thirty-five-year-old man recalled how he was favored as a child.

"I was always favored over my four sisters because I was the boy. I remember my mother saying to my sisters, 'Get off the couch, your brother wants to lay down.' For my graduation from high school, I received a car. My sisters each received a watch. I didn't think

I was being favored back at the time but now, as an adult, I feel so awful for my sisters and so guilty that I never tuned in to how they must of felt being less favored. I don't think my parents ever realized what they were doing to us."

SOLUTIONS

The first step to overcoming favoritism is to analyze your situation and see whether or not your child's unhappiness is the result of favoritism in the family. You need to ask yourself, very candidly, whether you are in fact favoring one child over the other(s). The following set of questions has been designed to help you determine your response. Answer **yes** or **no** to each one.

Do you think you are favoring one child over another?

Do you see yourself criticizing and scolding one child more?

Do you see yourself overreacting and yelling at one child more?

Do you punish one child more?

Do you give your other children more second chances when they misbehave?

Do you sense within yourself a dislike for one or more of your children?

Do you feel that one child irritates you more than the other children?

Do you feel it is hard to be openly loving to one of your children?

Do you find yourself labeling your children so that one is labeled positively and the others negatively? For example, she is my "angel" and he is my "little troublemaker."

Do you find yourself responding with sarcasm to one of your children?

If your "yes" answers have you wondering if you are favoring one child over the other(s), you need to take one more step to be sure. I want you to ask relatives for their frank and honest opinions as to whether or not you are favoring one of your children. If you don't have relatives available to ask, then contact your close friends for their candid observations. But first you have to reassure your relatives or friends that you will not hold their truthfulness against them. This is a hard thing for a parent to do, but you must—otherwise the consequences of favoritism will be severe for you as well as your child. *Favoritism is obvious to relatives and friends; it's not so obvious to parents.* For precisely this reason you need to obtain the objective observations of others.

Once you have concluded that you are, in fact, favoring one child over another, don't despair. Most parents are shocked to find themselves in this position, but it's not an unusual situation. Parents really do want to change their behavior once they realize the harm their favoritism has caused. The following two quotes reflect the reactions of two parents, both of whom acknowledged that they had favored one of their children:

"It suddenly hit me. I was packing my suitcase and the suitcase of my son for our third trip to Disney World when I realized that I had never taken my daughter to Disney World. How could I have been so cruel to this child. In the past I just told her she was no fun and off I would go with my son, leaving her behind. I can't believe I was favoring one child like this and being so unaware of the hurt I was putting my daughter through. I really need your help to figure out how I got myself into this situation."

"I have four children. It was Christmas Eve and my husband and I were placing our gifts for the children under the tree. As usual I had done all the Christmas shopping. As the presents began to pile up under the tree, I suddenly began to cry. Every child had ten to twelve presents, except my daughter Rachel. Rachel had three presents. My husband and I looked at each other in disbelief. I called my mother that night and told her about the presents. She began to cry and said she had seen me favor the other children for years, but did not want to interfere. My mother was so relieved to hear that I had become aware of what I was doing to my daughter. Can you help me make things right with my daughter?"

If you now realize you have a problem with favoritism, congratulations for having the courage to face it. The second step in solving this problem involves discovering what is good about your "bad child." To accomplish this task, I want you to do the following:

- Start listing the positive traits and qualities in your less-favored child. Take a couple of days to do this while you begin to observe your son or daughter more closely. You may discover certain talents and interests you had not seen before. Or you might discover how valued your child is as a friend.
- Schedule a meeting with the teacher of your less-favored child. Tell this teacher that you just want a general update on your child's performance in school. During the meeting, ask the teacher what she sees as strengths in your child. Most likely your child's teacher likes your child for a variety of reasons. You want to discover why your child appeals to other adults. In this way you can tune in to positive qualities you have been missing in your child.
- After your child has played at a friend's house, ask the friend's mother how your son or daughter behaved. This will give the friend's mother a chance to talk about all the good things she sees in your son or daughter. Again,

you are looking for how your child appeals to other adults. This will help you to appreciate qualities you may have been missing.

- Be sensitive to the compliments other adults give you regarding your child. In other words, work on changing your attitude about your less-favored child. Focus more on what other adults admire about your child and not on the faults you find in him.

Next, try to become aware of some shortcomings your *favored child* has. No child is perfect. You need to begin to see your favored child in a more objective light. This will help you have a more balanced view of your favored child. He is not perfect. He is like your less-favored child, a mix of strengths and weaknesses.

Start establishing new rituals with your less-favored child. If you have not taken your son or daughter shopping with you, then such a trip is definitely long overdue. If you have not spent any one-on-one time together, then private time is what both of you need. If there is some special activity your child particularly enjoys, then ask if it's all right if you join in it with her. In other words, start relating to your child in new and different ways that show you care and that your son or daughter is extremely important to you. Do this even if you don't particularly like the activity and have to force yourself at first to participate. You have to spend some quality time with the child who feels less favored if you hope to establish a positive connection with him or her.

Become more physical with your less-favored child. Even though at first it may be uncomfortable for you, it is vital to begin touching, hugging, and kissing your less-favored child. Add some meaningful compliments to these interactions. Be honest and forthright with your child. Kids can sense insincerity.

Love your children for the special and extraordinary people they are. In this sense, your love may not be equal among your children; it's an acknowledgment of their individuality and uniqueness.

Be very careful of quick reactions to your less-favored child that might repeat patterns of favoritism. After years of being biased against one of your children, you will tend to respond negatively out of habit to your less-favored child. You want to catch yourself and break this habit. Don't hesitate to apologize to your less-favored child when an apology is appropriate. If there is something about your child that really bothers you, think about why you are bothered by this characteristic. Oftentimes a problem in your childhood might render you sensitive to some particular behavior from one of your children. Your daughter may be aggravating you because she reminds you of a sister you hated. Your son's mannerisms may remind you of your former husband. I have found that this is frequently a problem among divorced woman who experience an intense dislike for their ex-husbands. In cases like this, a mom has to be very conscious of not blindly viewing her son as a smaller version of his dad. He may have some traits and mannerisms like his father, but very often the mother projects the prejudice she expresses toward her former husband onto her son. For example, a divorced mother may say about her son, "He lies just like his father." Well, most children lie. To say he is lying like his father is a projection on the mother's part. I recommend that divorced mothers with sons list all the traits and mannerisms their sons have that they believe come from the father. Once this list is complete, I ask the mothers to take each one and question whether there could be any explanation other than "he is his father's son." Next, I remind these divorced mothers that they are the ones who chose this man to be the father of their children. I point out that it is not fair to punish a child just because he has some of the genes from this man she now despises. In this type of confrontation I can appear rather harsh. But sometimes it is necessary to shock a mother into realizing that she has to make the effort to be fair to her son and not always associate him negatively with a man she no longer loves or respects.

When I was in training to become a child psychologist, one of the questions my supervisor asked me at times was "Why don't you like this child?" This is a terrific question to ask a future psychologist because a good child therapist must understand why some children bring up negative feelings while other children are so appealing. Parents are faced with the same challenge. Wise parents strive to understand their negative responses to a child within the family. They must always keep in mind that their child's well-being is at stake, and what parent wouldn't want her child to feel better, be better, do better?

If after three months you still feel discouraged with your progress toward alleviating favoritism, consult a child psychologist and a family therapist for help. There is nothing wrong in asking for help when you're stuck. I have counseled many parents once they became aware of their favoritism. Most were able to change their parenting behaviors with the help of counseling and to develop a positive and loving connection with their once less-favored child.

Stay in touch with your spouse or partner and relatives for feedback on how you are progressing to solve your problem of favoritism. The support of loved ones is crucial as you strive to change your parenting behavior.

SUMMARY

Everything I have asked you to do to overcome your favoritism is difficult. But the rewards for sticking with it and ultimately reestablishing a loving and meaningful relationship with your son or daughter are many. You will relieve the guilt you feel for having made the mistake of favoritism. You will relieve the guilt your other children feel because they have been favored. Your less-favored child will have the chance to heal and live a normal, happier life. And you will have a stronger family and the comfort of knowing you are a good parent.

RESOURCES

To learn more on how to help your child, I recommend the following readings:

The Emotional Problems of Normal Children: How Parents Can Understand and Help, by Stanley Turecki, MD (New York: Bantam Books, 1994).

100 Ways to Build Self-Esteem and Teach Values, by Diana Loomans and Julia Loomans (Tiburon, CA: H J Kramer, 1994).

Parenting from the Inside Out: How a Deeper Self-Understanding Can Help You Raise Children Who Thrive, by Daniel J. Siegel, MD, and Mary Hartzell, MEd (New York: Penguin Putnam, 2003).

What All Children Want Their Parents to Know: Twelve Keys to Successful Parenting, by Diana Loomans with Julia Goday (Novato, CA: New World Library, 2005).

CHAPTER 7

PERMISSIVE PARENTING

INTRODUCTION

There are many different ways to parent a child. Over the past twenty-five years, many parents have joined the ranks of permissive parenting. They may have settled on being permissive because they feel it is harmful to scold, punish, and train children to behave. They many have settled on being permissive because they believe loving a child is enough to make a child want to obey and cooperate. They may have settled on being permissive because they feel guilty when they make their child upset with discipline. Or they may have settled on being permissive out of a sense of being just plain exhausted by the demands of life and giving in just seems easier.

THE PROBLEM

Permissive parenting has been around long enough for us to now assess how effective it is in preparing children to run their own lives as adults.

The consensus among teachers, college professors, and employers is that **permissive parenting does not work**. Giving in to children may be easier, but the resulting problems for parents and young adults make life anything but easier.

Permissive parenting results in parents who are unhappy and children who are unhappy. In a home where permissiveness prevails, it is not uncommon to hear parents complain: *"These kids are driving me crazy!"* And children are unhappy because they end up being poorly equipped to deal with the real world. Mom and Dad may be permissive, but the world outside the home is not permissive. I recall a college commencement speech by Bill Gates in which he warned his audience that "life is not divided up in semesters with two-month summer vacations and your employer will not care about how you feel."

Despite the grief that goes along with permissive parenting, some moms and dads remain addicted to this parenting style even when their children have entered college. They continue their permissive ways right into the college years. "Helicopter parents" is the new phrase for permissive parents whose children are now college students. These parents, much to the annoyance of college officials, hover over the campus, cleaning up their "children's" dorm rooms, doing their laundry, balancing their checking account, editing their term papers, arguing with professors over grades, and waking their "children" for classes with early morning cell phone calls.

I think the best way to appreciate what permissive parenting is like is to look at actual, real-life examples of such parents in action. The following examples are from my own counseling sessions.

1. A five-year-old boy returns home on the school bus from kindergarten. As he comes down the steps of the bus, he is greeted by his mom, who is so excited to see him. As this little boy leaves the bus he has a frown on his face and, without warning, kicks his mother. Though the kick is painful, the mom in this situation said to her son: "Robert, why are you so angry, you know it's not nice to kick your mom."

Notice that no limits are set by the mother. The child is not scolded. No attempt is made to impress upon him that his behavior is completely inappropriate and will not be tolerated.

2. A couple have been invited over to their friends' house for a Saturday night dinner. They arrive dressed appropriately for a formal evening and with a bottle of wine for the host and hostess. Dinner is served in the dining room at 9:00 PM. To their surprise, a play table has been set up along the dining room table with two small chairs so their four-year-old and five-year-old can join everyone for dinner. Needless to say, the guests had little time to talk with their friends because they were constantly distracted by their young children. By the time dessert was served, the two small children had left their little table to play under the dining room table. The parents thought their children's silly play and banging into the feet of their guests was cute.

If these parents were not permissive, they would have recognized that parents need adult time. Permissive parents tend to not draw clear boundaries between adult time and time with the children.

3. Two parents arrive at a home for an engagement party with their three children, ages seven, ten, and eleven. There are only adults at the party, but since the invitation did not state adults only, they brought their children with them. The large dining room table was beautifully arranged with a wonderful buffet, offering a wide range of delicious foods. As the guests began to line up for the buffet, the front door bell rang. It was the deliveryman from a local pizza parlor with a large pizza. The organizers of the engagement party were confused since they did not order any pizza. They soon discovered that the mom who brought her three young children to the party ordered the pizza because her children only eat pasta, pizza, and burgers. The children turned their noses up at the food being offered.

Permissive parents constantly cater to their children, even in situations that are insulting to others. The correct response would have been for the parents to inform the children that there is plenty of food on the table for them to pick and choose. If they don't want to eat, then that is their decision, but special food is certainly not going to be brought in to accommodate them while at someone else's home.

4. A six-year-old boy defies his mother's request to clean up his toys, so she sends him to time-out. Without a hint of any annoyance or frustration in her voice, she

sweetly tells her son to choose one of his favorite story books, go to time-out, and to stay there until he feels he is ready to come out.

Time-out is not supposed to be a pleasant experience that the *child* controls. Permissive parents are forever abdicating their authority to the child.

5. Two parents are halfway through their dinner when Dad calls out to his five-year-old son and seven-year-old daughter, who are eating in front of the television, "I think it would be nice if you two would join us at the table."

Permissive parents often make weak requests when they need to be direct and clear. "I think it would be nice if you two would join us at the table" invites and encourages the children to say no. In this situation, the parents want their children at the dinner table but state their request in a way that allows the children to think that eating in front of the TV is an option. Besides, the children have been allowed to eat away from the parents for some time before the parents decided to make this feeble attempt to bring their children to the table.

6. Here is an example from my own office. While I was meeting with two parents, my office door suddenly opened and a six-year-old dashed into the room. This little guy was totally unaware that he had interrupted three adults in a private session as he ran over to the toy counter to play. The mother at this point was

standing in the threshold of the door and saying in a rather pleasant, singsong kind of way, "Dougy. Dougy, what are you doing? Now you come over here. Dougy? Dougy, did you hear me? Dougy, Dr. Condrell is going to be mad at you."

This definitely was a permissive mom. In this one episode the mother demonstrated so many of the behaviors that characterize permissive parents. She tolerated his inappropriate behavior to the point where my session came to a stop. She did not physically intervene to retrieve her son, allowing him time to get his own way playing with the toys. And of course, this little boy never received a clear message from his mother that he was bothering other people. Then this mother did what we so often see with permissive parents. She gave her authority away. Instead of saying in a firm voice that she was upset with him, she said, "Dr. Condrell is going to be mad at you."

These examples clearly identify some of the classic characteristics permissive moms and dads demonstrate. Rather than asserting their authority, they abdicate it. They do not take charge, opting instead to indulge their children's whims. When children act inappropriately like the little boy kicking his mom, there is no feedback that the behavior is unacceptable. Permissive parents tend to provide little to no feedback to their children regarding how their behavior impacts on other people. And permissive parents tolerate poor behavior from their children. Patience for parents is a virtue. But permissive parents extend patience beyond reason. They put up with poor behavior for extended periods of time at the cost of their discomfort before ever attempting to set a limit. And then the limit is most often so weak that the children do not respond. For example, a permissive parent bothered by the children's behavior might try to put a stop to their annoying behavior by saying, "Do you children want to stop?"

I have found that children raised in a permissive home are unhappy for the following reasons:

- Their home life is often chaotic. The children do what they want when they want, often ignoring their parents' requests to listen.
- Their parents often are not having a good time parenting because the children do not respect their authority and yelling is the only way they can get the children's attention.
- Planned family activities often fall apart because the children do not listen.
- The children do not have the security of knowing that their parents are in charge.
- The children are not prepared to succeed in school where rules, being respectful, and obeying the authority of the teacher prevail.

Children from permissive homes often are dismayed that other adults do not respond to them like their parents. And they often interpret the behavior of nonpermissive adults as "mean." You will often hear these children complaining that a teacher or a neighbor was "mean" to them. Any adult setting a limit or being firm or criticizing them is mean.

THE CHILDREN SPEAK

The following are characteristic statements made by children, ranging in age from five to eleven, to their permissive parents:

"You're not the boss of me!"
"I don't have to listen to you!"
"You can't make me!"
"This is your house not my house, so why do I have to clean up?"
"You are just a butthead, Mom!"
"You are such a jerk, Dad!"
"I'm going to call 911 and report child abuse!"

———

A nine-year-old asked the following question of his teacher:

"If this is your job and you get paid, how come we have to do all the work?"

———

A seven-year-old made the following statement to her sitter:

"I'm going to tell my mom you won't let me and she will fire you."

———

There is an old saying, "children do not know what is good for them." And this is true with the problem of permissive parents. Children do not know permissive parenting is bad for them. Children do not openly complain that their parents are permissive. And children do not openly express feelings of insecurity or unhappiness because their parents are not in charge. What I see, and childcare workers around the country observe, are children who are unhappy as a consequence of their permissive home lives. We see children in our offices who are unhappy because very little is working out for them.

- Their parents frequently are screaming and yelling at them to listen.
- Their teachers are often reprimanding them, putting them in time-out or sending them to the principal's office.
- They lose out on fun family experiences because the picnics, visits to amusement parks, and trips to zoos end up in chaos.
- Their teachers do not favor them because they are often poor students and disruptive in class.
- They feel put upon by classroom tasks and homework because of their lack of self-discipline.
- Their peers avoid them because they have so much trouble sharing, playing fair, taking turns, and not being bossy.

It is easy to see why children from permissive homes are often unhappy. They just can't verbalize the unhappiness or make the connection between their difficulties in life and how they are parented.

One word captures what these children are often like. That word is *BRATS!* It is a harsh word, but it communicates how these children come across to others. No one likes children who are brats!

SOLUTIONS

Become Aware of Your Parenting Style

If you have an unhappy child, she may be unhappy because of the way your parent. The first step is to see whether or not you are a permissive parent. These parents share some common characteristics. Check to see how many of the following characteristics apply to you. Ask yourself these questions:

- Am I often slow or do not recognize how my child's poor behavior is having a negative impact on other people?
- Do I view parenting as a popularity contest? Do I become hurt when my children get upset with me?
- Do I talk too much? Permissive parents have a strong need to have long persuasive discussions about why their child should comply with them.
- Am I too patient? The permissive parent absorbs way too much abuse from his children and way too much poor behavior before deciding to stop the inappropriate behavior.
- Am I inconsistent? Do I stop my child from misbehaving one minute and then the next instant give in or overlook the very behavior I just disapproved?

- Do I tend to "save" my children from the logical consequences of their actions? A permissive parent will always make an extra trip to school for forgotten lunches, assignments, and books even though the child has been irresponsible about such things for months. The logical consequence is the discomfort that occurs with forgetting lunch, school assignments not turned in, and demerits for not changing for gym class.
- Do I believe that just loving my children is enough to promote in them a strong character and self-discipline?

If you have answered yes to three or more of these questions, then you may well be a permissive parent. Complete the following questionnaire to be absolutely sure.

PERMISSIVE PARENT QUESTIONNAIRE

- Do I feel like my child is running me?
- Does my child talk back to me, speak disrespectfully, and call me names repeatedly?
- Does my child rarely take no for an answer and hardly ever cooperate with requests?
- Does the thought of making my child unhappy cause me to hold back from disciplining him?
- Am I reluctant to spoil what little time I have with my child by upsetting her with discipline?
- Does it break my heart to see my child upset when I set limits and have to say no?
- Do I believe that being a boss to my child hurts her self-esteem?

- Do I feel I spend too much time talking and explaining to my child, trying to persuade him to cooperate?
- Am I often embarrassed in public by my child's behavior?
- Do I worry that any mistake I make as a parent will result in permanent damage to my child?
- Do I have to ask my child ten times to do something?

If you answered yes to four or more of the questions and share three or more of the characteristics of permissive parents, you most likely are a permissive parent. If you are, don't be discouraged. You can learn to make your children and yourself happier by taking charge of your family. The following solutions will help you.

Convince Your Children That No Is No

Convincing your children that you mean what you say is your first challenge. If you are like most permissive parents, the word *no* has come to mean *maybe* and many times your no was changed to a yes. Children are tremendously perceptive people, and it doesn't take them long to catch on to the fact that Mom and Dad do not mean what they say. Permissive parents often cave in after they have decided to punish their child. I believe if you know the six most common ways children have of manipulating parents to cancel a punishment, you will be in a stronger position to stand your ground and not change your mind. Here are five of the ways children get their parents to give in to them.

1. Crying and Whining

Many children cry when the rules are enforced. Some even sob hysterically. Giving in to a child crying in response to some limit or punishment is a sure way of creating a perpetual crier. Your child will cry every time you don't back up your rules because she will have made a crucial connection, "I cry and I get my way."

2. Breath-Holding

This is a scary strategy some children use. Most parents cave in when their child's face begins to turn blue. I recommend that you stay calm at these times and don't rush to give in to your child. Experts say that nature will take over and force your child to breath. Some experts advise that you might distract your child, or tickle him, or do something unexpected to startle him the moment he goes into his breath-holding routine.

3. Threats

Children often will try to threaten you into changing your mind. "I'm never going to love you anymore," or "I'm going to run away," or "you will be sorry" are fairly common threats. Some divorced parents are so upset at the thought of losing custody when their children threaten "I'm going to live with Daddy" that they rarely stick to a punishment. And now we have the savvy kids who think they know how to play the "child's rights" card and threaten to call social services or 911 to allege abuse? This seems rather sadistic, but no doubt many try it, believing that they can harm their parents if they don't get what they want.

4. Making Parents Feel Guilty

Children make many guilt-provoking statements to push their parents' emotional buttons. "You're a mean mommy!" "If you loved me, you wouldn't do that!" "You're not fair." "You love my sister more." These statements are very effective in many homes and make parents feel so guilty that they back off from the punishment they just issued.

5. Begging for Just One More Chance

Making a deal and/or begging for one more chance is very common. Again, if you give in, you sabotage your parental authority. You probably have already given your child "one more chance" ten times over, so why fall for this one again?

———

As of this day, expect your child to cry, hold his breath, threaten, make you feel guilty, or beg for another chance when you enforce a punishment. Just knowing that your child will try one of these ways to encourage you to give in will give you the strength not to cave in when setting limits.

Not changing your mind and not giving in are giant steps toward establishing your authority with your children.

There isn't a parent around who has not given in to a

child. It is very difficult to set a limit and stick to it when you have a child cry or plead or promise to do better. Giving in from time to time doesn't mean you're a "bad" parent. But if giving in is a pattern, your child will quickly learn that you don't mean what you say. The most important point to remember is that you can still be a loving parent even though you are being firm about the limits you set and the rules you enforce. Permissive parents often think they are being mean when they try to be firm. These parents also worry about damaging their child emotionally or undermining the love their child has for them by being firm. I assure you that good parents are not mean when they set limits and good parents do not lose the love of their children when they stand their ground on a punishment. Permissive parents need to remember two slogans:

CHILDREN NEED DISCIPLINE IN ORDER TO DEVELOP SELF-DISCIPLINE

A PARENT'S JOB IS TO PARENT THE CHILD SO THE CHILD IS PREPARED AS AN ADULT TO FUNCTION SUCCESSFULLY IN SOCIETY

Make Your Rules Simple and Clear

Permissive parents are generally vague about their rules or make up rules on the spur of the moment. The next step toward changing from a permissive parent to one who is the leader of the family is to come up with a set of rules that have consequences. In a two-parent home, both parents must make the rules together so they are in agreement. The best way to think about what a rule should be is to consider those times within the family that are the most troublesome. For example, let's say in your family dinnertime is a problem. The children do not want to come to the table when you call them or they come but then repeatedly leave to play.

RULE

Everyone is expected to be seated at the dinner table for dinner when called. Dinnertime for the children is twenty minutes, and then they can be excused from the table.

Consequences:

- Not coming to dinner when called results in the child's plate being put away when the timer goes off in twenty minutes. The next meal is breakfast.
- Coming to the table and repeatedly leaving results in mealtime being ended for that child when she fails to listen to her parents' second warning to not leave the table. The next meal is breakfast.

This rule and the consequence of missing out on dinner strike most permissive parents as quite harsh, if not downright cruel. As a result chaos at dinnertime continues each evening. If you feel this rule is too harsh, then just say the following statement to yourself:

"I will only have to follow through on these consequences for a couple of evenings before the children realize they must respect this rule for the welfare of the entire family."

In other words, children catch on very fast when parents takes a stand and mean what they say. You will have to endure a scene or two for a couple of evenings and then the children will start obeying your rule that everyone is to come to dinner and stay for twenty minutes.

———

Another troublesome time for parents is bedtime. I recommend you make a rule for bedtime and also have a consequence. Rules must have consequences if they are to work. An example of a bedtime rule is:

RULE

As soon as homework is done, baths are taken, teeth are brushed, and pajamas are on, then there will be free time.

The message in this rule is the faster you get everything done for bedtime, the more time you will have to watch TV, play video games, and so on. What makes this rule work is the consequence. The consequence is that there will be no fun time until everyone is ready for bed.

Every parent needs to make a specific set of rules and decide on a specific set of consequences. Since this will be hardest for the formerly permissive parents, I recommend that they start out with no more than three rules. In my experience counseling families, I have noticed that permissive parents find it much harder to be firm. Trying to implement too many rules too fast can overwhelm them. My advice is to go slow and ease into your new role with respect to discipline. A step at a time can work wonders. As you succeed with a couple of rules, then add on another.

Learn the 1-2-3-Magic Discipline Strategy

You have learned that a no is a no. You have learned the importance of having rules with consequences. The next step is to have a strategy for inspiring your children to listen to you the first time. There are many discipline strategies that are available to parents, but the one I like best is Dr. Thomas Phelan's 1-2-3-Magic discipline strategy. This strategy works because it relies on time-outs. Time-outs remove a child from being involved with the family. This temporary isolation is a powerful incentive motivating children to cooperate. Dr. Phelan has taken time-outs to a new level of sophistication by giving parents a program for using time-outs that children cannot manipulate.

The next time your child is doing something you don't want him to do, try following this procedure. First, calmly give a warning that is both *verbal* and *visual*. You hold up one finger and you say that is 1. If your child doesn't stop, you give a second *verbal* and *visual* warning by holding up two fingers and saying, that's 2. If your child stops the undesired activity, that's great, but don't expect him to, because he hasn't in the past. If your child disobeys, you hold up three fingers and say, "That's 3, take 5." Your child then has to go to his room for five minutes. At the end of the five minutes, your child is allowed out. At this point be sure to:

- not lecture
- not apologize
- not be upset
- not talk and talk about how he is wrong and how frustrated you are

This strategy is so simple that most parents are in disbelief when they are instructed on how it works. Here are some of the most common questions parents raise about 1-2-3 Magic and my responses.

This strategy does not give children a chance to express their feelings or to consider the reasons for setting a particular limit. Don't children deserve an explanation?

Children deserve explanations on some issues, so their input at times should be respected. But the rules of the household are determined by the parents. The child knows in advance what these rules are. They are not negotiable. For example, rules like homework time is right after dinner, bedtime is 7:30 PM, and no television in the morning until after you are dressed and have breakfast are not open for discussion. There is a very simple guideline I encourage parents to recite to their children.

> "There are times we will discuss things so we can listen to your ideas and feelings, but there are other times when there will be no discussion on some matters because we know best."

We have put our son in his room and it not only didn't work but it caused more trouble. He became upset, had a temper tantrum, and cried and banged on the door. What can we do?

Children who are used to having their own way rebel when their parents set a limit and stick to it. So your child in this situation will try all sorts of things to reestablish that he is in charge. Keep in mind that one time-out does not change a child. Discipline is a process and the 1-2-3 Magic strategy will take a few weeks to take effect.

How long do you take between counts?

You say one, then wait five seconds. Then you say two and wait five second, and then three.

What if our child won't go to his bedroom?

You take him even if you have to pick him up.

What if our child will not stay in his room?

You hold the door shut and not say a word.

Do you ever make the time-out longer than five minutes?

For older children (ages eight and above) you can extend the time out up to twenty or thirty minutes for more serious behaviors. But do not do this often. It is best to keep most of the time-outs in the five- to ten-minute range.

What if my child goes right back and starts misbehaving?

Your child is testing to see if you really are going to be consistent and do what you say. Probably in the past you haven't, and he knows it. So when your child starts to misbehave again, you just go through the steps of 1-2-3 again.

———

1-2-3 Magic has had a lot of success in helping permissive parents to establish their authority with their children.

Consult a Child Psychologist and Family Therapist

If you find yourself stuck and can't seem to assert yourself with your children, then you should consult a child psychologist and family therapist. This is a service in which most child psychologists are experienced. I personally have helped many parents gain control of their families. Generally, I start by having a couple of sessions with both parents to assess their situation and to get them thinking about rules and consequences. Then I have a couple of family sessions where the children attend. It is during the sessions involving the children where the parents introduce their new rules, the consequences, and express their desire to change things at home. When a professional is consulted, the parents have the advantage of being reinforced and empowered to make the changes they need to make. Also the children hear from the professional that their parents are correct in wanting to make things better at home. A family doctor or a pediatrician can guide you to find an experienced family professional.

Should Children Fear Their Parents?

A chapter on permissiveness would not be complete without addressing an issue that concerns permissive parents. "Isn't it bad for children to fear their parents?" This is the issue that concerns many permissive parents. It is this issue that prevents permissive parents from becoming more firm, more structured, and more consistent with their children. Early in my career, I concluded that children should not be brought up to fear their parents. I began however to reconsider my conclusion, after I had made about one hundred presentations to parent groups. I found that almost all parents in every presentation I gave raised their hands when I asked if they grew up fearing their parents. Not only did parents raise their hands, but, in retrospect, almost all the parents in my audiences supported their parents. I was stunned by their responses. I began to seriously rethink this issue of kids fearing their parents by interviewing parents on what they feared as children. Their responses were both interesting and consistent. They did not fear being hit or punished. They feared disappointing their parents, or letting their parents down.

One evening while attending a lecture by Gen. Colin Powell, the general spoke of his own childhood and fearing his parents. As he talked of his youth, he commented how he had this fear inside of him that had to do with not letting his parents down, or not disappointing his parents. Powell was at a loss however to explain how his parents had inspired this fear in him. To my surprise, the talk brought back a memory from my own childhood. My family, too, were immigrants. Powell's parents came from Jamaica and my family came to America from Greece. Like the general, I also grew up feeling that the worst thing I could do was to disappoint my parents. I do not know how this idea was planted in my mind, but it was there up through my early adult years. After hearing General Powell speak, I revisited the question of: *Is it bad for children to fear their parents?* As I thought about this question, I reframed the question to communicate more clearly what parents were telling me and what Powell had related to his audience. The reframed question asked: *Should children have an apprehension about letting their parents down, or disappointing their parents?* What follows is the sequence of my thoughts in response to this question.

Normal children are in love with their parents.

Normal children from their earliest years want to impress their parents with their achievements and their behavior. "Look Mom, look Mom, look what I can do" is a statement filled with excitement that parents hear over and over again.

Children's love for their parents inspires them to strive to impress their parents with their growth, achievements, and social skills.

Children sense their parents' expectations and the standards they want their children to meet.

Why isn't it a good thing, then, for kids to be apprehensive of letting their parents down?

I came to the conclusion that it is a good thing for kids to not want to disappoint their parents, that this apprehension, worry, or whatever you want to call it, can be inspiring to children. I believe children should worry about disappointing their parents much like they worry about winning when they play competitive sports or failing an exam in school. A certain amount of worry is good for kids. It helps motivate children to try their best.

THE GOOD NEWS

I see a trend today of some parents going back to raising their children the way they were raised, with expectations clearly stated, high standards, and good values. I do not believe parents have to fear that they will be damaging their children by setting firm limits, offering a structured home life, being consistent, and following through on consequences.

SUMMARY

It is very easy to overlook permissive parenting as a cause of unhappiness in children because on the surface, giving in to children seems to make them happy. In reality, permissive parenting exposes children to feelings of insecurity, family chaos, frustrated parents, and poor preparation for dealing with peers and school. This is what causes the unhappiness. If you are a permissive parent of an unhappy child, this chapter can give you the basics for establishing your authority as a parent. Don't put off helping your unhappy child. Any hope you have of achieving a harmonious family life will depend on it.

RESOURCES

If you want to learn more about how not to be a permissive parent, I recommend the following books:

Children Who Do Too Little, by Patricia H. Sprinkle (Grand Rapids, MI: Zondervan, 1993).

The Epidemic: The Rot of American Culture, Absentee and Permissive Parenting and the Resultant Plague of Joyless, Selfish Children, by Robert Shaw, MD (New York: HarperCollins, 2003).

The Manipulative Child: How to Regain Control and Raise

Resourceful, Resilient, and Independent Kids, by Ernest W. Swihart Jr. and Patrick Cotter (New York: Random House, 1998).

Raising a Child Conservatively in a Sexually Permissive World, by Sol Gordon, PhD (New York: Simon & Schuster, 1983).

1-2-3-Magic: Effective Discipline for Children 2–12, by Dr. Thomas Phelan (Glen Ellyn, IL: Child Management, 1984).

Parent Power: A Commonsense Approach to Parenting in the 90's and Beyond, by John Rosemond (Kansas City, MO: Andrews and McMeel, 1990).

Parents Who Love Too Much: How Good Parents Can Learn to Love More Wisely & Develop Children of Character, by Jane Nelsen, EdD, and Cheryl Erwin, MA (New York: Random House, 2000).

Wimpy Parents: From Toddler to Teen—How Not to Raise a Brat, by Kenneth N. Condrell, PhD, with Linda Lee Small (New York: Warner Books, 1998).

CHAPTER 8

STEPFAMILIES

INTRODUCTION

Many years ago, a single father I was counseling walked into my office to tell me he had remarried over the weekend. He was bursting with excitement. This father couldn't wait to tell me all about the wedding and how he surprised his three children. He had told his children that he was taking them on a picnic. They knew nothing of any wedding plans. After arriving at the park, the father and the children hiked up a hill, then through a small forest of trees. The children expected to see a picnic table and swings on the other side of the trees. As the children emerged from the trees, however, what they saw were 150 white folding chairs, a trellis covered with flowers, a crowd of people, a minister, and Dad's girlfriend dressed in white. Within the hour she would be their new stepmother. Dad surprised the children with his good news that they now would *all be a family again*. Like many newly remarried parents, this father was in love and filled with optimism about the future. Several weeks later, he returned to my office to tell me that his three children did not share his excitement about being a family. In fact, they were really upset that he married a woman they did not want to be their stepmother.

Each year, millions of divorced parents happily remarry, only to find that the children are not at all happy about the new state of affairs. Since many remarried parents have no idea what challenges lie ahead of them, they spend little, if any, time planning how they will handle the new relationships, different personalities, and unforeseen issues facing their new family. I find that most remarried parents feel confident that their love will get them through whatever tough times they may encounter. But when it comes to stepfamilies, love is not enough; and that is why 66 percent of these families end in divorce. Of all the family structures we have today, the stepfamily is the one most likely to self-destruct. Nevertheless, divorced and single parents are joining their families at the rate of thirteen hundred new marriages a day according to Patricia L. Papernow, author of *Becoming a Stepfamily*. In fact, the United States now has more stepfamilies than first-married families.

THE PROBLEM

When parents remarry, we say they have formed a stepfamily or a blended family. I like the sound of "blended families" better, so I will use this term to refer to families in which parents have remarried. There are different kinds of blended families. A dad with children marries a woman with none. A mom with children marries a childless man. A dad with children marries a mom with children. Parents with deceased spouses marry. Coupled parents form new partnerships. And sometimes a dad with children marries a mom with children and they then go on to have their own children.

Blended families also vary with regard to how friendly or hostile the ex-spouses are to the new marriage. The makeup of blended families of course also varies with the ages of the children. Sometimes the children are all teenagers and sometimes they are young children or middle school children or a mix of preschoolers and high school students. No matter what combination of ages exists in a newly formed blended family or what kind of blended family a couple creates, all these families have one thing in common: the new family structure presents remarried parents with more opportunities for conflict than any other family situation in existence today. And this poses problems for the parents and for the children. The potential for unhappiness throughout the family is enormous.

In a natural (or what I will sometimes call a normal or a traditional) family, adults fall in love, marry, become husband and wife, and go on to become mothers and fathers. In today's world there are many variations of the natural family, as I have described. But all natural families have one thing in common: the children represent a part of each parent. So in the normal natural family, the birth of the children usually energizes the parents to develop a deeper bond. The birth of children brings the parents closer together. In a blended family the partners merge their respective families into a new, larger one. The children are already there. In fact, the children are often part of the wedding ceremony. But unlike the children in the natural family, those who come into the blended family often pull the parents apart. Children in a blended family have the opposite effect of children born into a natural family. And this is why blended families are so much at risk for all sorts of emotional conflict and turmoil.

The following statements were made by remarried parents who were in the early stages of their blended family. Note the types of recurring problems these parents face in their blended families.

"I was only married six months when I heard my eight-year-old stepson ask his mother why she ever married me. I listened and heard that not one of my wife's three children wanted me as their stepfather. I felt unbelievably hurt and also trapped. I had committed myself to a second marriage with children who didn't want me. I felt I had failed again."

———

"He expects me to be their mother, but he interferes when I try to be their mom.

"The first twelve months were horrible. I tried so hard to be the perfect wife and mother, but his children resented everything I did for them. In front of their father they acted like little angels, but when he wasn't there they treated me awful. And of course my husband didn't believe me when I asked for his help. He thought the kids were doing great with me."

———

"My husband seemed so interested in my son when we were dating, but now he has very little to do with him. My first husband abandoned us and I thought, finally, my son would have a real father, but Ed isn't emotionally involved with my child. I don't know how much more of this I can take."

———

"She sees things they do that I never see. I feel she is overly critical of my children."

———

"There is always a tone of nastiness when she talks to my children."

———

"I never thought I was the jealous type, but twice a month my wife meets with her ex-husband over lunch to discuss the kids. It's great for the kids that they get along, but I'm upset that she leaves me at home to go meet with their father. It just bothers me."

———

"I was so eager to meet Ellen's family. But there I was forty years old and feeling so rejected. All her father did was talk about Ellen's first husband and how wonderful he was with the kids. Her brother and sister looked at me like I caused the divorce. It wasn't at all like I imagined. I expected warm, accepting in-laws, but what I got was the deep freeze, and I haven't even married Ellen yet. Do you think this will get better after the wedding?"

———

"He criticizes me in front of his children and then they on purpose don't listen to me. They actually grin when he puts me down for disciplining them."

———

"His four-year-old daughter said her mommy called me a slut. And then she asked me, 'Anne, what is a slut?' How am I ever going to get close to his children if their mother is using words like this to put me down?"

———

"My son came over for his weekend the other day and said his mother told him I was sleeping with Liz before the divorce. I didn't know what to say to him. His mother had lied to him, but I didn't want to put her down. Besides I feel so uncomfortable talking about stuff like this with a seven-year-old. It looks like my former wife is going to do whatever she can to disrupt my new family. I'm so upset!"

"My children are so upset with me because I'm living with my stepchildren and they only get to see me a few hours each week. I really see their point. I feel so guilty in the evenings as I sit around with Mary's four children and my children are miles away. I really didn't think it would be like this. I love Mary and I'm so happy with her, but there is a hole in my heart for my children."

"I thought my wife would be such a great mom to my daughter, but since we settled down in her house, she treats *my* daughter like Cinderella and *her* two daughters like princesses. I feel like such an outsider in Claire's house. It is *her* house and not *our* home. Both my daughter and I feel like intruders rather than part of the family. Claire has changed so much since the wedding."

"My husband and I now fight every time a holiday approaches. We never have all our children together for the holidays because of having to share them with the other parents. There are times when the kids don't want to leave our home and I see the sadness in their faces as we get them ready to leave to be with their dad or mom. How can you have a family when every weekend it's musical chairs with kids coming and going between homes?"

———

"We fell in love and had this fantastic relationship. I thought this could only get better when we were all under one roof and a family again. How could I have been so wrong? The last three years were hell."

THE CHILDREN SPEAK

For years I have been listening to children tell me about their remarried parents and how they feel about their stepparents. As you listen to what these children have to say, focus on the kinds of issues that cause these children to feel unhappy in their blended families.

"I want my dad to be around every day, not Charlie. Charlie is nice, but he's not my dad. I hate my mom for getting rid of Dad and marrying Charlie."

An eight-year-old boy said this to me after his mom had remarried. I met this little boy when his mom brought him to me after she found two of her nightgowns cut with a scissors. Her son, Alex, later confessed to me that he did the cutting. He also apologized to his mother. I asked him why he did this and he said, " I hate what my mom has done to my life."

A thirteen-year-old girl talks about her mother's remarriage:

"From the time my parents told me they were divorcing, I imagined them getting back together. After the divorce, I imagined them coming to my birthday party and making up. Sometimes I imagined that I would get very sick and be in the hospital. My parents would come to see me and be in the same room again and fall in love. I had these dreams right up until my mother walked down the aisle. Every time I see my stepdad now, I feel this empty feeling like my parents will never be married to each other again."

After both of his parents recently remarried, this ten-year-old boy reacts to his new family situation:

"After my parents divorced, my life was never the same. I thought things just couldn't get any worse, but they did. My mom married this jerk, and my dad married this lady who is always bossing us around. She even makes us go out to play when we would rather stay inside. It is so stupid. My parents made themselves happy and they made me miserable and they do not seem to care. Sometimes I feel like running away."

"I want things the way they used to be," complained this nine-year-old girl about her new family. "I want my old family back. I don't care if Mom and Dad fight. It was better then than it is now."

———

When asked how his life had changed since his mother remarried, this six-year-old boy complained:

"She is always paying attention to him and not us. She lets him tell us what to do. He is not my real dad, but my dad is busy with his new family. I just hate all this."

———

A terribly unhappy eight-year-old boy who had become exceptionally close to his mother during her single-parent years, now faces life in his new family:

"How come Ray gets to sleep with you and I don't. How come you leave me to go out with him and I have to stay home without you?"

———

"I hate my stepmother," said this ten-year-old girl. "She never yells at her daughters and she is always picking on me."

———

For this eleven-year-old girl, it's her stepfather who's the problem:

> "My stepfather is not my father, and I don't have to listen to him. My father says that he better not yell at me or punish me."

———

Since his dad remarried, this seven-year-old boy complains about how his life has changed:

> "Ever since my father got married, he never has time to do things with me. He always brings his new wife and her kids along."

———

This nine-year-old boy talks about being caught between his father and his stepfather:

> "I really like my stepfather a lot, but my father gets real upset if I do something fun with my stepfather. Dad says my stepfather is a jerk. I don't know what to do. I started lying to my dad about how I'm not spending time with my stepdad."

———

Here a twelve-year-old girl has turned against her step-mother:

> "My mom says my stepmother is a slut and that Dad was sleeping with her while they were married. I hate my stepmother now 'cause she broke up our family."

———

Here stepsiblings are the focus of this eleven-year-old girl's anger and resentment:

> "I like my stepmother, but her kids are brats. I can't stand them. They always try to get me in trouble."

———

> "Every time my dad does something for me," this seven-year-old boy remarks, "his wife complains that he is ignoring her kids. She keeps spoiling our time together."

———

Clearly, blended families provide fertile ground for childhood unhappiness to take root. When children become unhappy in these newly created families, the kids look unhappy, they pout, and they are often tearful. These children can become argumentative, belligerent, sarcastic, defiant, disrespectful, and uncooperative. Frequent displays of temper and a drop in their school grades can also occur.

SOLUTIONS

The solutions I am presenting here represent some of the best advice I can offer to parents who want to succeed with their blended families.

Become Aware of the Pitfalls of Life in a Blended Family

No one is prepared to succeed as a stepfamily unless they learn why this kind of family is so unique and so prone to problems. Even if you are in the midst of a lot of conflict in your new family, it is not too late for you and your spouse to educate yourselves on life in a blended family environment. There are many ways for remarried parents to survive and enjoy their new blended family. But one requirement is crucial: *both parents have to be on the same page regarding how the children will be managed and disciplined.* To accomplish this, *both parents* have to *educate themselves* on blended families. In this way, each parent will begin to develop more compassion for what the other parent is experiencing. Both parents will also become aware of the problems they have to work together on to solve. This chapter will get you started. (For more information on blended families, I call your attention to the list of resources at the end of this chapter.)

To begin this educational process, I'm going to start with the seven most troublesome areas in a blended family. Parents need to have this information because chances are one or more of the children in your family will become unhappy as a result of these trouble spots:

- The ex-spouses are hostile to the new marriage and inspire their biological children to resist the new blended family. My experience has been that hostile ex-spouses are generally not a little hostile. They are often very hostile. Therefore, I recommend parents consult a family counselor. This situation calls for expert help. You need someone who can analyze the dynamics of your family and offer customized strategies.
- The children are faced with adjusting to a nonbiological parent and to children from another family who are now their stepsiblings. I suggest parents begin this process before the marriage by spending one-on-one time with the other parent's children and by planning fun experiences where all the kids are together. After the marriage, family counseling may be necessary to work out conflicts among the children and conflicts between the children and the parents.
- The parents need to meet and communicate with the ex-spouses regarding the parenting of the children. I recommend choosing a meeting place that will not inspire jealous feelings from your new spouse.
- Relating to the first set of in-laws for the sake of the children while becoming involved with the new in-laws. If you love the first set of in-laws, this will not be much of a problem. However if the in-laws took your ex's side, you are going to need to practice self-control. Remind yourself as you approach the unfriendly in-laws that you are enduring this experience because it benefits your children.
- The scheduling of the children so they can leave the

home of one parent to be in the home of the other parent for weekly visits, holidays, or summer vacations. A huge calendar hung on the wall, with visitation days clearly marked, can prevent confusion and reduce stress.

- The loyalty conflicts the children experience for their biological parent as they begin to like or fall in love with their stepmom or stepdad. I advise biological parents to give their children permission to like and love their stepparent.
- The financial stress of supporting a new family while paying child support and or alimony to a former spouse. Consulting a financial planner is a wise step to take as you launch your new family.

In my experience, these seven trouble spots are the most common sources of unhappiness for children. By being aware of them, parents are in a better position to focus in on what may be causing a child in the family to be unhappy.

Consult a Family Therapist

If you don't find the reading materials on blended families to be helpful or clear, then consult a family therapist. These professionals are experts on remarried families, and they can teach you what you need to know to start taking the steps toward improving the relationships within your new family. Look upon your family therapist as your coach. She will listen to what you are going through and coach you and your spouse on how to work together to solve your problems.

Don't Expect Too Much Too Fast

It takes time for a new blended family to come together and function like a traditional family. There are a lot of adjustments to be made on everyone's part, and this cannot take place in a couple of months. Some families require years. It's best to lower your expectations of having one big happy family right away and take things one step at a time.

Recognize There Are Six Stages That Blended Families Must Pass Through in Order for the Members to Function Like a Traditional Family

Blended families grow, and, just like children who must endure growing pains, these families go through various stages of maturity. Patricia L. Papernow, author of *Becoming a Stepfamily*, states in her research with these couples that there are six stages remarried parents or newly coupled parents pass through with their children. These stages are like a road map. They help parents to see where they are in their development as they strive to blend their families to live together with some degree of harmony.

The first stage is the **Fantasy Stage**.* Single adults generally yearn to have a loving partner and a satisfying family life. This desire is so strong that single parents who decide to remarry or form a new partnership experience a great sense of optimism that they finally will have the happiness both have been longing for. In this stage, both partners dream of a

---

*While the descriptions of the six stages are the author's words, the names of the stages are from Patricia L. Papernow's book.

happy family life. They imagine a wonderful future since they love each other so much. Like most adults forming a blended family, they are not aware of the many problems they will have to deal with. Their optimism creates a cloud of fantasy that hides the realities they will face as their two households merge. In this stage, parents find their optimism turning into feelings of despair and confusion. "This is not the way I thought it was going to be" is a statement I often hear from parents who recently merged their families.

The second stage is the **Immersion Stage**. Here couples who have married or formed a new partnership come face to face with the many negative feelings their children have about their new family. The children in a blended family have a natural bond with their biological parent. This powerful natural bond causes children to feel resentment toward the new stepparent who tries to parent them and jealousy over having to share their own biological parent with the stepparent and the stepparent's children. Problems like these and many others involving the children soon explode the fantasy of being one big happy family. The immersion stage completely bursts the bubble of one big happy family. The stress in this stage is so intense for parents. They face three possible realities: divorce, family counseling, or resignation to living an unhappy home life.

The third stage is the **Awareness Stage**, in which the stepparent accepts the reality that there is no instant family. Divorce is not an option and living in conflict is not an option. The parents become aware that it will take time to work through all the feelings the children have about their new family. In this stage, the biological parent also becomes aware that there will be no end to the problems in the family unless both partners form a strong parental team to run the family. It is during this stage that the parents, feeling hopeful, become more united as a parenting team with a renewed spirit of working together.

The fourth stage is the **Mobilization Stage**, at which point the couple openly airs differences between step and biological family members' needs. This is an intense stage with a lot of battles. Here the biological parent feels torn between the spouse's needs and the children's needs as the spouse becomes more vocal. At this point the adults negotiate new agreements about how the family will function. In this stage, they develop a full awareness of the issues they face, so that every family activity no longer becomes a power struggle. By the end of this stage, couples are feeling relief. They have established agreed-upon rules and limits for the children. The children begin to respond more cooperatively as they see the chaos and turmoil diminish between their parents. "I feel like there is light at the end of the tunnel" is a statement I hear from parents as they approach the end of this stage. "We are beginning to feel like a real family" is another statement parents have expressed to me as this stage winds down.

In the fifth stage, the **Contact Stage**, the children have been pushed out of the relationship the adults in the family have with each other. If the adults are married, then we say that, in the contact stage, the children are no longer in the middle of the marriage. The boundaries have been clearly established where the parents are now a true couple and a solid parenting team. During this stage the children stop playing one parent against the other, and stepparents develop real relationships with their stepchildren.

The sixth stage is the **Resolution Stage**, at which the step relationships no longer require constant attention. Instead, they function well. The family has reliable step relationships and a solid family history begins to develop.

An awareness of these six important stages helps parents to see where they are and where they have to go. I suggest you use these stages like a map to chart your progress toward creating a normal, functioning family.

Give Your Children Permission to Love Their Stepparent

It is so unfair for Mom to be able to fall in love with her new partner and for Dad to be able to fall in love with his, but the children are not allowed to fall in love with their new stepparents. This happens all too often in remarried families, and it makes children very unhappy. It is human nature for biological parents to feel threatened when another man or another women becomes involved in raising their children. Biological parents feel scared of losing their child to another adult or of having their relationship watered down. Parents can solve this very personal and emotional problem by recognizing that your relationship with your child will always be special and unique. As a parent, you are not going to lose by giving your children permission to love their stepparent. You simply say to your child:

"It is really okay for you to love Harry. You won't be hurting my feelings. Our relationship will always be special." Or "I think it is wonderful that you like Elizabeth. She is a nice lady, and my feelings will not be hurt if you have good times with her. Our relationship will always be something very wonderful just between us."

In my practice I have actually had parents face their child and deliver messages just like these. You can't imagine how relieved the children are to receive this permission. It relaxes them, eases their tension, and makes them very happy. They no longer have to keep their feelings for a stepparent secret or act like they don't like their stepparent just to please Mom or Dad.

This simple strategy of giving your children permission frees them to be natural and spontaneous in both homes. This may not be easy for you to do, but it will make a world of difference for your child. Children need a lot of love from many different adults in their lives such as parents, grandparents, aunts, uncles, godparents, and stepparents.

Be Cautious about Your Children Tattling on Their Stepparent

Children are often very manipulative in a newly formed blended family. They will do everything possible to strengthen their relationship with their biological parent while sabotaging the new marriage. This includes lying, making up stories, and distorting what really happened between them and a stepparent. Imagine how you would feel if your daughter came up to you and said, "*She's* always yelling at my *dad* and she lets *her* son get away with everything." Because of problems like this, I recommend that the adults in the family should always get both sides of the story before reacting.

31-01 20th

Long Island City,

Prepa

PAR

290 Elwood I

Liverpool, N

Phone: (3

Fax: (31

Expect to Be Rejected by a Stepchild

You might be wondering just how helpful it is to be advised to expect rejection. It's more helpful than you realize. When you expect to be rejected, you put yourself in the position of not being shocked and of not overreacting when it occurs. And chances are it will occur. But difficult as it will be, try not to take the rejection personally. Most likely it's not you. More often than not it's the situation that the child is rejecting and it wouldn't matter who the stepmother or stepfather was. Children generally just don't like seeing their parents remarry. Many kids have told me that seeing their parents remarry is just a "weird" experience for them. What kids mean by weird is seeing their parents being romantic and sexy. Biological children tend not to be so aware of their parents' sexual relationship.

As you live with your stepchild (or stepchildren), keep two thoughts in mind:

- Every child of divorce secretly wishes their parents would reunite and *you* just spoiled that fantasy by marrying her parent.
- No child of divorce is eager to share his parent with a new wife or a new husband. In the child's mind, this only means he will receive less attention from his parent.

These two thoughts will help you feel empathy instead of anger for your stepchild. So expect to be rejected. And by all means, do not retaliate by rejecting your stepchild. If you do, the child will surely feel justified in declaring war, and much unhappiness for everyone in the family will follow. In many cases, a few gentle talks and one-on-one time will solve the problem.

Reach Out to Your Stepchild

All to often parents make the mistake of doing everything as a family. Being a family is fine and advisable, but stepparents need to bond with their stepchildren and win their trust and respect. This means you will have to spend one-on-one time with your stepchildren. Your stepchild (or stepchildren) may resist your interest in spending time with her, but don't back off. I have seen many children experience closeness with a stepparent they at first resisted going out with. This special time can work like magic in creating a bond between children and their stepparent.

Avoid the "My Children" Trap

This is a tough one. By the time you remarry, you and your children have been through a great deal and you are very close. Naturally, as a loving parent you feel protective of your children. In the early stages of a blended family each parent thinks of biological children as "my children." It takes quite a while before a couple can talk about "our children." The following tips will help you avoid the "my children" trap.

Stepmoms have to expect that when Dad's children come for their usual time with Dad, he will be overly attentive to them. Most dads do not live with their children, and they miss them very much. Therefore, a stepmom has to be sensitive and not complain that "you ignore my children when your kids come over" or "you act like my children don't exist when your children arrive." It is far better for a mother to recognize how her husband misses his children and to say to him before a visit: "I know how much you have missed your kids. Do you think that after you do something with them you can spend some time with all the children?"

Do Not Go to War over Disciplining the Children

This is another tough one. So often in a blended family the husband feels that his wife is too strict with his children, and the wife feels that her husband is too permissive with his children. Another scenario would be one in which the wife feels her husband has been too harsh with her children while allowing his children to manipulate him. I recommend that both parents decide what the rules, consequences, routines, expectations, and chores will be for *all* the children. Each parent will have the right to remind the children of the rules or their chores or that it is homework time, but only the biological parent should enforce the rules of the family with his or her biological children. This is especially important for the first year and maybe longer. In such situations each blended family is different. For example, if the remarried family started off with teenagers in high school, then most likely only the biological parents will enforce the rules. If, however, the remarried family started off with very young children, most likely both parents would equally enforce the rules after a few months of transition time. I also recommend that the parents meet as often as necessary to discuss their feelings regarding discipline in the home. Sometimes rules and chores need to be changed, and sometimes each parent may feel offended by the way the other parent approaches the children. These situations need to be discussed immediately when the children are not around.

Avoid the "Super Stepmother Complex"

This is a problem many remarried women experience in a blended family. As a woman falls in love with her future husband, she begins to hear all sorts of stories about the biological mother. Usually these stories are negative, and in time the soon-to-be stepmother comes to be as critical of the biological mother as the ex-husband. And she starts to think, " I will be the mother these children never had." Unfortunately, this view fosters a competitive relationship with the biological mother. The new wife finds herself on a mission to be the best possible mom to the children, both to please her husband and to please her stepchildren. The trouble with this well-meaning attitude is that most kids will hate the quick and intensive intrusiveness of their stepmother in their lives. And in many cases they will feel threatened that she is trying to take their mother's place. In no time at all, the stepmother feels martyred. All she wanted to do was please her husband and be the best possible mom to the children, and now everyone is mad at her. To avoid this trap, a stepmother should never become competitive with the biological mom. Whatever shortcomings the children's mother may have, *she* is their mother and their only biological mother. The stepmother needs to remember this and not set out on a campaign to improve the children's grades, manners, and responses to all her new rules.

Do Not Let the Children Hear You Argue about the Ex-Spouses

The challenge for a blended family is to have all the children come to trust and bond with the new parent. Stepparents must keep in mind that when they put down the biological parent, they end up shooting themselves in the foot. Children will almost always be protective of the biological parent. My advice is to keep your conversations private when they focus on the parents outside of your blended family.

SUMMARY

There are many experiences beyond the awareness of parents that can cause children to become unhappy. The structure of the blended family offers a child many experiences that can cause considerable unhappiness. Parents who remarry or form new partnerships are wise to educate themselves and learn as much as possible about blended families. In this way you will be able to anticipate problems and respond in ways that will heal rather than hurt. I encourage you and your spouse to learn together as you strive to make your blended family the family you dreamed of during your courtship.

RESOURCES

There are a number of Web sites that offer advice to stepparents. Two Web sites you might want to explore are:

http://www.stepfamily.org

http://www.successfulstepfamilies.com

There are also many books out for remarried parents. Here are some books I consider very helpful.

Be a Great Divorced Dad, by Dr. Kenneth Condrell with Linda Small (New York: St. Martin's, 1998).

Becoming a Stepfamily, by Patricia Papernow (San Francisco: Jossey–Bass, 1993).

The Courage to Be a Stepmom: Finding Your Place without Losing Yourself, by Sue Patton Thoele (San Francisco: Wildcat Canyon Press, 2003).

Positive Discipline for Blended Families: Nurturing Harmony, Respect, and Unity in Your New Stepfamily, by Jane Nelsen et al. (Rocklin, CA: Prima Lifestyles, 1997).

Step-by-Step Parenting: A Guide to Successful Living with a Blended Family, by James D. Eckler (Cincinnati, OH: Betterway Books, 1993).

Step Coupling: Creating and Sustaining a Strong Marriage in Today's Blended Family, by Susan Wisdom, LPC, and Jennifer Green (New York: Three River Press, 2002).

CHAPTER 9

SIBLING ABUSE

INTRODUCTION

"Mommy, Mommy, he hit me!"

"I did not."

"Yes, you did."

"Tyler, how many times have I told you not to hit your sister?"

———

"You always take *her* side," Aaron screams as he storms off to his room. "You never listen to *me*! You love her more than me."

Slam!! The walls shake as Aaron bangs his bedroom door shut.

Sound familiar? Conflict between siblings is the most common source of tension in the majority of families. Professionals label this problem "sibling rivalry." This simply means "competition." Sisters and brothers compete against one another in order to achieve a more favorable position in the eyes of their parents. The prize, of course, is more attention, more love, and a sense of greater status within the family as the most favored child.

Children start off wanting their mothers all to themselves, but most soon learn they have to share. Mommy doesn't just belong to Kevin. Mommy is married to Daddy, so Kevin must learn that he has to share Mommy with Daddy. Then, when a little brother or sister arrives, Mommy has to be shared even more. Children struggle all their young lives with the difficult concept of sharing and feeling jealous. All this of course is quite normal and expected as children develop and mature psychologically and emotionally.

THE PROBLEM

Every parent is familiar with sibling rivalry, but most parents are totally unaware of *sibling abuse*. This type of very negative relationship between siblings is not normal. Sibling rivalry becomes sibling abuse when one child is always the victim and another child is always the aggressor. Sibling abuse is the consistent bullying and mistreatment of a brother or a sister. In my experience the abuser:

- is frequently an older child who has little or no love for the younger sibling
- resents the presence of the child he or she victimizes
- doesn't miss a chance to humiliate, demean, or hurt the victimized sibling

- is unrelenting in cruelly mistreating the victimized sibling
- continues to reject the victimized sibling well into adulthood

There are certain specific situations in a family that can increase the possibility of sibling abuse. Parents need to recognize these risk factors. Here are four of the most common risk factors:

- one or both parents are absent from the home for considerable periods of time
- the parents are at a loss as to how to handle sibling rivalry in the family
- the parents are unable to stop one sibling from being violent toward another sibling
- one sibling is overburdened with caring for a brother or a sister

In our society, parents expect fights to occur among siblings. They view this as the natural working out of differences between two or more unique individuals whose efforts of self-expression will inevitably clash—at times rather aggressively. Because of this, sibling abuse is often not recognized by parents, no matter how attentive they are to their children's needs. In my practice I have repeatedly listened to parents describe to me incredible nastiness by one sibling against another and then writing it off as "kids being kids."

The problem is clear: *When abusive acts occur between siblings, most parents do not perceive them as abuse.* Unlike child abuse or sexual abuse perpetrated by adults, there are no legal reporting requirements for sibling abuse. Consequently, hospital staff, when examining a sibling with cuts, gashes, or severe bruises, generally dismiss it as normal and make no report.

Clinical experience indicates that sibling abuse can result in strong, long-lasting effects on the victimized child such as:

- profound feelings of inferiority
- depression and anxiety disorders
- alcohol and drug addiction
- eating disorders
- feelings of insecurity and social withdrawal
- failure in attaining career goals
- post-traumatic stress disorder

In my practice, I generally do not see cases of sibling abuse until the teen years, between the ages of thirteen and seventeen. It is during this time of intense physical, psychological, and emotional development that parents bring in their teen to see me and express great concerns about his or her lack of confidence and self-esteem. Upon examination, I often discover that the teen does not merely lack confidence but actually *loathes* herself. As I explore the dynamics of the family, I often discover that the teen is the victim of sibling abuse. I am always amazed that the parents are not at all concerned about their abusive son or daughter. For these parents, the idea of sibling abuse never entered their minds as a potential source of conflict in the family.

It is, in fact, a huge problem. By the time I see these victimized children as teenagers, they are absolutely convinced they are utterly worthless. In their eyes they are no good and have no redeeming qualities. When I compliment these teenagers for the strengths I see as I observe them during our sessions together, they dismiss my remarks as contrived attempts to be nice because that's my job. It is as if they *know* they are worthless, and no one is going to convince them otherwise. Many perceive themselves as having little or no inherent worth because they have been brainwashed by the abusive sibling day after day, year after year. Imagine yourself as the target of a persistent campaign of derogation and all you hear about yourself constantly is how you are no good or stupid or you can't do anything right. In time you will come to despise yourself. And that is exactly what happens to women who are abused by their husbands or male companions and to men who are abused by their wives. In such abusive situations, both children and adults emerge harboring profoundly distorted self-images. Is it any wonder that many abused children and teenagers seriously consider suicide? I am not at all surprised since most, if not all, of the children and teens I have seen who I suspect to be victims of such abuse have been depressed for years.

Sometimes the abuse takes on an added dimension when one of the parents in the family, for one reason or another, is not emotionally available to the victimized child. For example, if a brother is abused by his older sister and the father is absent from the home for weeks at a time, the child concludes that he has not only been rejected by his sister but by his father as well. In this child's eyes, this rejection could only occur because *he* is worthless. It is unthinkable to a young child that something could be wrong with his father or his older sister. *The problem has to be his. He is the one who is unlovable.* Once this kind of thinking takes hold of the victimized sibling, that youngster often begins to act in self-defeating ways. He punishes himself by sabotaging successes and sets himself up to lose because he doesn't deserve any better. The perceived rejection resulting from the father's absence, coupled with the actual rejection by a sibling, leaves little room for any other conclusion than there is something wrong with me. This kind of thinking over time leads to further distorted thinking in the victimized child. The child actually comes to believe he is so bad he is totally undeserving. This self-hate and self-loathing is very powerful in the mind of an abused sibling.

THE CHILDREN SPEAK

Good parents are compassionate. They easily place themselves in their children's shoes and feel what they feel. Many parents, however, fail to appreciate how awful it is to be an abused sibling.

A young man of twenty talks about his years as an abused sibling:

"My brother was three years older than me. I used to live in fear of him. When I heard his steps, I used to hide. He constantly punched and kicked me and called me names. My parents would tell him to stop and tell me he really loved me. Growing up in that house was hell."

———

Abuse of one sister by another is no less intense than their male counterparts as this nineteen-year-old woman shows when she speaks about her abuse at the hands of an older sister.

> "My sister tortured me all the time when were kids. After we grew up, we remained enemies, and when she died, I did not even go to her funeral."

———

> "I believed everything my brother told me," said a twenty-three-year-old woman during one of our counseling sessions. "I was dumb, ugly, and no one would ever love me or marry me. You can't believe the problems I have now trying to make a life for myself."

———

Here a high school boy of sixteen talks about the abuse he endured from his older sister:

> "I'm sixteen years old now and my twenty-three-year-old sister still slaps my face and looks at me with such disgust. I try to avoid her and not upset her, but it doesn't help. My parents have just given up on getting her to stop. I have been out of school now for six months. I just can't seem to have the courage to take any teasing at school, and I'm seeing a counselor."

———

I have found that children and teens victimized by a younger or older sibling frequently describe themselves in the following ways:

"I'm just a loser."
"Everyone is better than me."
"I'm nobody."
"I feel I'm ugly and stupid."
"I can't do anything right."
"I really hate myself."

SOLUTIONS

1. Learn to Recognize Sibling Abuse

Parents must first make themselves more knowledgeable about the problem of sibling abuse. Here are some key questions to ask yourself if you have an unhappy child you suspect is being abused by a sibling.

- Does the child make spontaneous comments about hating himself or hating his life?
- Does your child show signs of physical injuries that may take days to heal or require medical attention?
- Does the child you are worried about avoid his sibling?
- Is your child submissive to her sibling?
- Does your child appear to fear a sibling?

- Is one sibling relentlessly calling her brother or sister insulting and degrading names?

If you answered yes to at least three of these questions, your unhappy child may be the victim of sibling abuse. Now check to see if the following behavior patterns are evident in your family:

- The aggressive sibling shows little to no affection for the sister or brother he is picking on.
- The aggressive sibling shows no guilt or concern for how nasty she is to the brother or sister she is picking on.
- The child who is picked on often asks his parents why the aggressive sibling hates him.
- The picked-on sibling craves the approval and affection of the aggressive sister or brother but is almost always rejected and ridiculed.

If two of these behavior patterns are evident in your family and you have answered yes to at least three of the questions listed above, then it is most likely that sibling abuse is present in your family.

2. Set Ground Rules to Prevent Abuse

Once parents are aware of sibling abuse in the household, they must take a very firm stand when confronting the aggressive sister or brother. A rock-solid ground rule must be established that there will be no teasing, belittling, intimidating, shoving, hitting, or name-calling in the family. The new family message is:

"In this family when we are upset with each other, we will not be mean to each other."

As we have seen in other chapters, for a ground rule to work, there must be meaningful consequences. For younger children a loss of fifteen minutes of their playtime before bed for every violation of the rule can be effective. For example, a nine-year-old sister could be going to bed an hour and a half earlier because she was mean to her younger brother six times in one day. For a teenager, a meaningful consequence could be losing weekend privileges and being grounded if, in the previous week, she did not show a significant improvement in her abusive behavior. Each family will have to work out the best consequences for the rules they set in their own situation.

3. Stop Giving Older Children Too Much Responsibility for Younger Children

If you suspect your older sibling of abusing his younger brother while you are not at home, it may be time to rely on an after-school care program for the younger son, no matter how inconvenient or expensive this may be for you.

4. Provoke Guilt and Set Standards for the Aggressive Sibling

There are times when it is necessary to make a child feel guilty. Usually in sibling abuse, the aggressive sibling has been aggressive for so long that his or her conscience has become numb. It is up to the parent in a one-on-one conversation to make the aggressive sibling feel guilty for what he is doing to his little sister. To accomplish this, a parent needs to be dramatic in portraying how the aggressive sibling is making the victimized child feel. A parent, for example, might say something like this:

> "Do you have any idea what you are doing to your sister? Day after day you make fun of her and call her gay, retard, butt face, and make fun of her. And when you are not humiliating her with these awful names, you are shoving her or tripping her. Do you know how this makes your sister feel? Your father and I are not going to tolerate this any more. It has to stop!"

If you have a two-parent home, I recommend that both parents meet jointly with the aggressive sibling. If that is not possible, one parent should confront the child. The other parent should follow up the next day with the same message. In a two-parent home, it is very powerful for both parents to deliver the same message to a child or teen.

5. Stop the Violence and Separate the Siblings

Parents should immediately intervene when physical violence occurs between siblings. Once the siblings are separated, they should be sent to their rooms for a cooling-off period, followed by a family meeting. The parents should direct this meeting by relying on three basic questions:

- **What happened?** Each sibling gets a chance, without interruption, to tell his story of what he perceived happened. After the parents have heard from each sibling, they can then ask questions to gather more information and details. The goal of this question is to piece together an accurate picture of what took place.

- **How do you feel about what happened?** The parents need to encourage each sibling, one at a time, to express how she feels. The goal of this question is to have each sibling fully express her individual feelings. It can be quite an emotional relief when feelings are expressed. At times the aggressive sibling might even experience appropriate feelings of regret and guilt when he hears the feelings of a brother or sister being expressed.

- **How will you handle this problem the next time it occurs?** The children need to work out a plan for avoiding a fight when the triggering event occurs in the future. This is a problem-solving time, one in which the entire family can join. It is also a good time for the parents to repeat the following message as the meeting comes to a close:

> "We are a family and no one will be allowed to hurt or mistreat any member of this family. We either solve this problem in the next few weeks or the whole family is going to see a counselor. This cannot go on."

6. Consulting a Family Counselor

As reasonable and helpful as it is for parents to set limits and consequences and for them to have family meetings in an effort to stop instances of sibling abuse, sometimes this approach just doesn't work. If you have not been able to stop the sibling abuse in your family, then I strongly urge you to meet with a family counselor. Your pediatrician or family doctor can direct you to an experienced professional in your community. You need to follow through with this recommendation because:

- the abused sibling can be damaged for a lifetime by this experience.
- the abusive sibling could maintain her pattern of abuse into adulthood and eventually mistreat her children and/or her spouse.
- the siblings could end up being lifelong enemies and miss out on the pleasures in life that come from having a loving and caring brother or sister.

No matter what the cost for counseling or how inconvenient it may be to take the whole family to sessions, it doesn't compare to the grief the entire family could suffer if the problem is allowed to continue unresolved. Sibling abuse is like a cancer. It can destroy a family and ruin the life of the abused youngster.

In my practice I often have a series of sessions with both siblings alone, without the parents, followed by a series of meetings in which both parents participate. Coming to a counselor usually impresses the abusive sibling with the seriousness of the problem. Counseling also gives the parents a chance to be empowered by a professional who uses his authority to make it very clear to the siblings that this problem is serious and that it has to stop. Often parents do not view the seriousness of the sibling abuse in the same way, and counseling can shed much-needed light on the gravity of the situation and the enormous risks it poses to both the children and the family as a whole, thereby assisting both parents in joining together to put an end to the problem.

7. Start Managing Sibling Rivalry More Effectively

Over the years, I have developed a five-step plan for minimizing sibling rivalry that I believe really works.

Step one. Sibling rivalry is caused by each child desiring to be your favorite. When parents arrange to give their children this special kind of experience on a regular basis, sibling rivalry quiets down. So each week go ahead and give in to your children's individual fantasies of being an only child. This is accomplished by spending one-on-one time with each child. The time can be as short as twenty minutes. During this time it is just you and that one child. If you're married, then each parent can rotate and the process becomes easier. Being able to spend private time with a parent once a week is emotionally soothing for a child, and you will love the experience, too. Private time helps to calm their jealous feelings. If you can commit to more than one session a week, then by all means do so.

Step two. Stop playing judge each time the kids get into a fight. Playing judge actually inspires your children to fight more. Let me explain. Since each child wants to be your favorite, the children are forever trying to get each other into trouble with Mom or Dad. So, when you play judge, you end up making one child the "good" kid and the other child the "bad" kid. The "good" kid sees himself as your favorite and the "bad" kid hopes the next time she will be able to turn the table on her brother. So you see, by acting like a judge, you are actually rewarding the fighting, which will continue and possibly even escalate. This is just the opposite of what you want. Instead of playing judge, inform your children that, starting tomorrow, there will be a new rule. Then explain that each time they start to fight, you will give them a two-minute warning to stop and find a way to get along. If they don't succeed, they will both be sent to their rooms for twenty minutes. Here is how it works.

Say to your children when they start to fight, "You have two minutes to stop and find a solution. If you don't, you are both going to your rooms for twenty minutes." Chances are the kids will shout back, "but that's not fair; he started it." You then answer back, "I don't care what is fair. All I know is that you have to learn to get along, and if you don't stop fighting, you are going to time-out for twenty minutes. At the end of the time-out, ask your children how they might solve the problem they had when it occurs again. They may have an idea, such as "I will play with the play station for fifteen minutes alone, and then he gets to play fifteen minutes," or you may have to supply a solution for them to try out next time. Remember, children have to learn to get along with others, and this process starts at home. As you teach your children how to work out disagreements, you are also teaching them how to get along with their friends.

Step three. Inform your children that after dinner you will make a decision on how successful they have been at getting along that day. Explain that if you see an improvement they will have their normal privileges after dinner. This means they will be able to play and watch TV and have their normal bedtime and routine. Think of a privilege as anything your child enjoys and looks forward to. If your children have behaved poorly with each other all day, they will lose their privileges and have to go to bed forty-five minutes early. If they do show improvement, then they have earned all their normal privileges for the evening. I understand that this may sound harsh to you. But being harsh is only temporary because most children respond to this approach in a week or two. The reason for approaching persistent sibling rivalry in a strict manner, as I have described, is because this is a tough pattern to change. A significant consequence is required to alter this pattern. It is a question of gaining control of the sibling rivalry or continuing to suffer day in and day out with the bickering and the fighting, along with the long-term damage it could be doing to the child who is victimized.

Step four. To further inspire your children to work on getting along, offer them a weekend prize. Inform your children that if you decide that they have had a good week, then they can have a weekend prize. You and the children then decide on Sunday what the prize will be for the coming week. It could mean renting a video, having a friend stay over, making popcorn, ordering a pizza, playing a special game they love, getting to stay up an extra hour, going to the movies, or going to the mall. Stop and think about this. Your children now have to cooperate in order to win a special activity they love.

Step five. Step five is very simple. You just catch them when they are good. What this means is that periodically you reward your children with your attention when you see them getting along. You compliment them for getting along. This is a very powerful strategy in helping to shape your children's behavior. Most parents ignore their children when they get along and yell at them when they start fighting. In this way, parents are giving the poor behavior attention and ignoring the really good behavior.

I suggest that for normal sibling rivalry you start off with steps one, two, and five. If you have a bad case of sibling rivalry, then you should do all five steps.

Just to make sure you understand how to minimize sibling rivalry, I will now tell you how to make the fighting in your home worse! Always do things with your children as a group. Never spend any alone time with each child. You can rationalize this by saying: after all, we *are* a family. When the kids fight, rush in and decide who was wrong and who was right, and yell at the kid who seemed to start things. When your children do get along, ignore them and say nothing about how nice they are playing. I'm being facetious here, but you get my point.

Severe sibling rivalry can make family life a nightmare and take all the joy out of parenting. These five steps can help you effectively manage sibling rivalry in your family and avoid the more serious problem of sibling abuse.

SUMMARY

Sibling abuse is a serious problem, often overlooked by parents. It can result in lifetime problems for the abused child as well as the aggressor. Your child's unhappiness could be your first clue that sibling abuse is occurring in your home.

RESOURCES

In my opinion, two of the best books for further reading are:

Sibling Abuse Trauma: Assessment and Intervention Strategies for Children, Families, and Adults, by John V. Caffaro and Allison Conn-Caffaro (Binghamton: NY: Haworth Maltreatment and Trauma Press, 1998).

What Parents Need to Know about Sibling Abuse: Break the Cycle of Violence, by Vernon R. Wiehe, PhD (Springville, UT: Bonneville Books, 2002).

CHAPTER 10

THE ANGRY PARENT

INTRODUCTION

Over the years, I have met many parents in my practice who were angry. Some were angry at their circumstances in life. Some were angry with the other parent for not doing more as a spouse and a parent. Some were angry over the frustrations they feel being a single parent. Others were angry about the frustration they experienced in their relationships with others. As I listened to these parents, I could understand why they were feeling angry, but these parents had not consulted me regarding their anger. In fact, many did not even know that anger was a problem for them. Instead, they had sought my professional advice because one of their children was in their eyes unhappy.

Anger is not an uncommon emotion for parents to experience. Parenting is difficult and it can tax the patience of the most even-tempered person. But parental anger that persists day after day, week after week, is not normal. This kind of anger is caused by factors other than the frustrations of parenting. Parental anger at this level is a major cause of unhappiness in children.

THE PROBLEM

Parental anger is a problem for children. First, children perceive their angry parent as a mean parent. Second, children believe they made their parent angry because in some way they have done something wrong. So children with an angry parent blame themselves for causing their parent to be angry and conclude that their parent is most specifically being mean to them. The following is a list of behaviors that characterize the angry parent.

Angry parents:

- lack patience
- overreact to minor problems and the mistakes of children
- yell and scream a lot
- say things to their children that are nasty or emotionally abusive
- are overly critical and fault finding
- do not plan enjoyable family experiences
- rarely give compliments to their child
- find it difficult to be nurturing
- are not fun to be with
- are generally cranky and irritable
- easily lose their temper

The child of an angry parent is generally exposed to all this negative behavior on a regular basis. In addition, the child living with an angry parent is pained by the belief that she is the cause of her parent's anger and that her parent is being mean to her. Knowing all this is important, because it helps a parent to understand why children become unhappy when they live with an angry parent.

Children generally respond in three ways to their angry parent:

1. Children interpret their parent's anger as proof that they have lost the love of that parent. "Mom doesn't love me" is a conclusion children often make when they live with an angry parent.
2. Children start copying their parent's angry behavior. Children are great copycats. They are forever copying their parent's behavior. So it is not at all unusual for a child with an angry parent to act just like that parent by overreacting, having temperamental outbursts, and being both verbally and physically abusive.
3. Children come to see their angry parent as being a mean person, and so they feel justified in being mean back. They become defiant and uncooperative and break rules on purpose. After awhile these children who live with an angry parent can actually lose their desire to please their parent.

So children living with an angry parent often respond by:

- concluding they are unloved
- copying the angry parent's behavior
- becoming defiant and uncooperative

Anger is a parent's worst enemy.

THE CHILDREN SPEAK

A seven-year-old boy expresses himself about his mother's anger:

> "Lots of time my mom is angry and so grouchy. She tells me to leave her alone when she is having a bad day, but every day is a bad day for my mom. I feel like she doesn't love me any more."

———

An eight-year-old boy expresses his unhappiness to me about living with his angry mother who is a single parent.

> "My mom is always angry. She always yells for tiny things. She has rough days. She always tells me when she has a rough day. Mostly every day is a rough day. She always argues with my dad. My dad never yells, but she thinks he yells. She sleeps a lot. She says, 'A mom's job is never done.' I feel lonely because my mother is lots of times asleep and there is nothing to do and she gets angry if I wake her. I feel unhappy most of the time because I feel like I'm doing something wrong."

———

An eleven-year-old boy expresses his feelings about life with his angry father. I asked this youngster to tell me what it is like living with his dad.

He responded. "It's a hell hole, my home is hell."

I asked him to tell me more and he said, "He embarrasses me to no end when he swears at me in front of my friends. He make me feel very small, little, like he controls me and I have no life. I feel like I don't want to do anything he wants me to do."

———

A four-year-old girl talks about her angry dad.

"I hate my dad."

"Why do you hate your dad?" I asked.

"Cause he's mean to my mommy. He's mean to all of us. He swore at my brother yesterday and now he won't talk to him. [Her brother is six years old.]

Then this little girl added: "Sometimes he's nice but he's mostly mad. He scares me. I don't want to be near him."

SOLUTIONS

In my office, I start helping angry moms and dads by first making them aware of what they often don't know or don't realize; that they have a lot of anger and that there is a definite connection between their anger and their child's behavior. I then show them how their anger is sabotaging their parenting. Some parents are relieved that I have found the problem that is causing them so much trouble and causing their child so much unhappiness. Some parents, however, turn their anger on me for making this connection and focusing on them, rather than their child. These parents often become indignant because in their eyes there is something wrong with their child and I'm now saying to them that there is actually something wrong in the way they are handling their child. Sometimes an angry parent will settle down and counseling is successful, but on other occasions this kind of parent storms out of the office with one more thing to be angry about and I never see him or her again, and the children continue to suffer.

RECOMMENDATIONS

The first step you need to take toward helping yourself and your child is to check yourself out to see whether or not you are an angry parent. You need to observe yourself to see if anger is sabotaging your parenting. This may sound like a strange recommendation. How can parents observe themselves? It's really not that hard. All you have to do is remind yourself that today you are going to become very conscious of how you are behaving as a parent. You start off each day psyching yourself up to be more conscious, more aware, of how you handle your child. You might even decide to keep notes to see how often you:

- yell or scream
- make threats
- overreact

- lose your patience and your temper
- become sarcastic or verbally nasty
- hug and kiss
- say "I love you"
- laugh and joke
- ask your child if you can join him or her in play
- compliment your child

Next, I want you to continue your self-examination by asking yourself the following questions. Take your time as you look over each question and be very honest with yourself:

- Is anger an emotion I experience easily and frequently?
- Do I feel cheated by life?
- Do I feel overworked, overextended, and overscheduled?
- Am I irritable and easily frustrated?
- Do I hear myself yelling at my children more than I want to?
- Do I feel guilty over my lack of patience with my children?
- Do I say harsh and nasty things to my child?
- How satisfying and fulfilling is my adult life?
- Do I feel like a victim?
- Do I swear at my child(ren)?
- Do I slap, push, grab, yank, spank, pull hair, and pinch?
- Are my children afraid of me?

After answering these questions and after observing yourself interacting with your children, ask yourself this question: "If I was a child again, would I want to have a mom or dad like me?"

If you conclude from your observations and self-analysis that anger is affecting your interactions with your child, then you need to rely on the following strategies to improve your parenting and to help your unhappy child.

Use "self-talk" to modify your anger. Self-talk is when you silently talk to yourself to focus on modifying your angry responses. For example, during the day you give yourself reminders with statements such as:

"I hear myself getting way too angry today. I need to calm down."

"I'm leaving work feeling angry and I have to be careful not to bring this anger home with me and spoil the rest of the day with my family."

"I can see my children listening better to me when I don't yell."

Here is another strategy for helping you to manage your anger and improve your parenting. I want you to make two lists. In one list you will write down all the ways you **wished your parents had treated you**. A list of wishes might start off with:

I wish my parents did not argue so much.
I wish my parents had hugged me more.
I wish my parents were not so critical of my school-
    work.

In the other list you will write down what you **liked about the way your parents treated you**. This list might start off with:

I loved the way my parents took me skiing.
My parents made sure I saw my grandparents every month.
We had dinner every night as a family.

Take a couple of days to complete these two lists because your memory needs time to recall past events. Once your lists are complete, look at them and review each item. Then combine your two lists into one. This master list will provide you with a plan for being a more nurturing and fun parent, and it will help your child to not associate you with your anger. The list will also be uplifting for you because it is made up of childhood wishes as well as special memories.

An additional strategy for managing your anger and helping your unhappy child is to focus on having more fun and more play experiences with your child. I have learned over the years that there is no better way to communicate to a child that he is loved than to play with him. We hug children. We kiss children. We tell them we love them. But the very best way to show a child that he is loved is to play with him. When we play with children, we emotionally connect with them and thereby establish a real closeness, a real bond. We are also saying to a child through play that we really value him and enjoy him and want to be with him. Children need to feel this message of love loud and clear if they are to grow and develop a healthy sense of who they are. All children need to feel special; they need to know they are valued and admired as individuals. Hugs, kisses, expressions of love, and taking the time to have fun are simple actions that parents can engage in, but they communicate an enormously important message to youngsters: that your child is very important to you and that you really do love him.

A few years ago, several child psychiatrists were asked for their best advice on how parents could inoculate their children from developing emotional disorders and being unhappy. These experts were unanimous in advising parents to play with their children. The exact prescription was for parents to play with each of their children on a one-on-one basis at least once a day for fifteen to twenty minutes.

Another approach to managing your anger is to ask yourself "How do I need to change my life so I feel more fulfilled and less angry." Anger is almost always a sign that something is not right. Find out what is not right and begin to work on it. Angry parents generally have a blind spot: they blame their children for their anger instead of looking within themselves for the source. In other words, most angry parents blame their children for their own unhappiness and avoid looking inward for answers. If you feel stuck in resolving your anger or in improving your relationship with your unhappy child, then consult a professional. There are many excellent therapists who can help you improve your life and your parenting skills. There are three major professional groups who offer counseling services: psychiatrists, psychologists, and social workers. I think one of the best ways to find a suitable counselor for yourself is to ask your family physician, pediatrician, or primary care provider. These doctors have considerable experience with mental health professionals in private practice and can direct you to a reputable counselor. There are two Web sites I recommend that can help you. One is http://www .LookandSeek.com. This site offers additional information on how to select a counselor. The second Web site is http://www.4therapy.com. This site is a therapist locator.

All health insurance policies these days must provide for mental health services. A call to your carrier will clarify the benefits you will receive from your policy.

Some parents find it helpful to repeat affirmations to themselves on a daily basis. An affirmation is a statement you make up to keep yourself aware of the problem you want to work on and to remind yourself of what you want to change. Here are some examples of affirmations a person might use if he has a problem with anger.

"Anger destroys personal relationships."

"It is important for me to control my anger so it doesn't control me."

"When I get angry, I almost always make things worse for myself and others."

"When I feel angry, I should think before I speak."

"I am a good person and I do not want to hurt others with my words."

"Anger is not going to fix the problems that get me angry."

It may seem silly to repeat statements like these during each day, but affirmations allow us to program our minds so we can behave differently. Computers can be programmed instantly by changing the software. Humans, however, can only change their thinking slowly over time by repeating new ideas and thoughts on a daily basis.

People who have anger problems usually overreact to situations and make mountains out of molehills. They obsess and fixate, thus turning many a "so-so" situation into a full-blown catastrophe. For example, it is very common for a person with an anger problem to say things like "Now everything is ruined" or "This is just awful" or "This whole day has been terrible" or "You can't do anything right." When people think in these exaggerated and dramatic ways, it's easy for them to experience anger. So, to help make a positive change in your life, you need to question yourself if you find yourself thinking in such a catastrophic way. For example, ask yourself "Is everything *really* ruined? or "Is it accurate for me to say that my son can't do anything right?" In other words, you need to begin to challenge yourself when you overreact to a situation and describe it as a disaster or awful.

SUMMARY

It is never easy to accept the reality that we need to work on ourselves. If by reading this chapter you are now aware that anger is interfering with your parenting, take comfort in knowing that you have made a giant leap forward toward improving your family life. The solutions offered in this chapter will help you to manage your anger better. You will find that as your anger intrudes less into your parenting, your children will become more loving and more cooperative. You will have stopped the vicious cycle in your home of your anger breeding anger in your children, which almost always turns kids into uncooperative, unhappy children. In a short time you will find that you have become more of a success as a parent.

RESOURCES

If you would like to learn more about managing your anger and how to parent an unhappy, uncooperative child, I recommend the following books.

Angry Children, Worried Parents: Seven Steps to Help Families Manage Anger, by Sam Goldstein, PhD, Robert Brooks, PhD, and Sharon Weiss, MED (Plantation, FL: Specialty Press, 2004).

How to Control Your Anger before It Controls You, by Albert Ellis, PhD, and Raymond Chip Tafrate, PhD (Secaucus, NJ: Citadel Press, 1998).

Screamfree Parenting: Raising Your Kids by Keeping Your Cool, by Hal Edward Runkel, LMFT (Duluth, GA: Oakmont Publishing, 2005).

Try and Make Me, by Ray Levy, PhD, and Bill O'Hanlon, MS, LMFT (New York: Signet Books, 2002).

What to Say When You Talk to Your Self, by Shad Helmstetter, PhD (New York: Pocket Books, 1982).

When Anger Hurts: Quieting the Storm Within, by Matthew McKay, PhD, Peter D. Rogers, PhD, and Judith McKay, RN (Oakland, CA: New Harbinger Publications, 2003).

Who's in Charge Here? Overcoming Power Struggles with Your Kids, by Dr. Bob Barnes (Grand Rapids, MI: Zondervan, 1997).

Wimpy Parenting: From Toddler to Teen—How Not to Raise a Brat, by Kenneth N. Condrell, PhD, with Linda Lee Small (New York: Warner Press, 1998).

CHAPTER 11

WHAT MAKES
A CHILD HAPPY

I t is my sincere hope that the previous chapters have created within you a greater awareness of the most overlooked causes of unhappiness in children. I am now going to shift the focus of discussion to raising a *happy child*. Here I will emphasize those emotional needs that must be nurtured in order for a child to be well adjusted and happy. I hope to provide parents with:

- a simple, easy-to-follow strategy for parenting well-adjusted, happy children
- a checklist of characteristics a family must have in order to parent a happy child
- seventeen powerful parenting guidelines for becoming a more effective parent

Generally speaking, unhappy children display a variety of behaviors that make them difficult to live with. Unhappy children:

- are often poor sports
- cry easily
- pout frequently
- whine
- rarely smile or laugh
- complain a lot
- are uncooperative
- are defiant
- are not desired by other children
- have behavior problems in school
- are disrespectful
- are pessimistic
- are not trusting
- are reluctant to try new things
- are not very thoughtful
- are emotionally distant

Many unhappy children are really not a pleasure to parent. Some tug at our heartstrings. I remember a little seven-year-old boy at the University of Michigan Fresh Air Camp. I was his camp counselor. His name was Ivy Lea. Ivy attached himself to me from day one. He used to come up to me and say: "You know, I bet if we went into Ann Arbor, everybody would think you were my daddy." I agreed with Ivy even though he was black and I was white.

One day I gave Ivy a photograph of himself as a gift. I loved taking pictures of the kids and giving out copies. In no way was I prepared for what happened when I gave Ivy his photo. Ivy became hysterical. He fell to the ground in a rage, sobbing painfully. We couldn't console him for about an hour.

Later that day, Dave Wineman who pioneered the camp, explained to me what happened. He said:

> "Ken, Ivy had a fantasy that you were the dad he craved to have. When you showed him your photograph, it tore his fantasy apart. He was confronted with the reality that he was black and you could not be his dad. All the hurt and anger locked up inside of Ivy from being fatherless exploded and overwhelmed him."

It has been forty-six years since I have seen Ivy. I still tear up when I remember this unhappy child. Since that day, I can spot fatherless children almost immediately just by the way they follow me around.

Happy children have very different characteristics and generally are enjoyable to be around. Children who are happy:

- smile a lot, act silly, and make jokes
- cooperate with parents and teachers
- make good companions
- are playful and love to use their imaginations
- show affection spontaneously
- are enthusiastic about life
- trust others
- are caring and thoughtful
- enjoy their friendships
- develop a passion for different activities
- explore their world

- play pretend games
- act confident
- love adventures

A happy child is a well-adjusted child, one who is a pleasure to parent.

What steps can parents take to ensure that their child will be well adjusted and happy? You have already taken a very important step by reading this book. Here you have learned what experiences and situations are toxic to children, thus causing them to become unhappy. The next step is to become more aware about a child's world and what must go on in this world for the child to grow up feeling good about himself and prepared to interact with others in constructive ways. What follows is a simple strategy for monitoring the life of a child. With this strategy parents will be able to assess how their child's life is progressing and, when necessary, to intervene to bring their child's life back into balance.

A child's world is made up of three parts:

- family
- school
- friends

If you want to discover what is making a child unhappy, you must search for problems in each of these areas. Likewise, if you want to learn what makes a child happy, you must know the essential experiences in each of these areas that empower the child to be emotionally healthy and happy.

EXPERIENCES ESSENTIAL TO A CHILD'S MENTAL HEALTH AND HAPPINESS

Family

Every child needs a family with at least one adoring adult, who will be that child's mentor, advocate, and cheerleader in life. When children feel desired, wanted, and important within their family, they have the emotional foundation necessary for learning all the lessons they need to learn about leading a meaningful and successful life.

- Children feel happy when they feel connected and loved within the families. That is why hugs, kisses, being held, snuggling, and expressions of "I love you" are so important to children.
- Children feel happy when their parents teach them to do things they couldn't do before. This makes youngsters happy because children love to feel grown up. And nothing makes a child feel more grown up than learning new skills and becoming more capable, competent, and independent with the help of a parent he or she looks up to and admires.
- Children are happy when their feelings are not hurt unnecessarily by the words their parents choose to correct them. Instead of hearing "you are a slob," they hear "your room is a mess and needs to be cleaned." Instead of hearing "you are lazy," they hear "you haven't done your chores yet." Parents are teachers, and good teachers teach children without sarcasm, insults, name-calling, and words that make a child think and feel unworthy.

- Children are happy when their family plays together and makes time for fun. Sledding, bowling, family movie night, games, flying kites, picnics, bike rides, swimming, and camping are just a few activities children love to do with their family.
- Children are happy when they can enjoy close relationships with relatives like grandparents, uncles, aunts, cousins, nephews, nieces, and godparents.
- Children are happy when their parents inspire and encourage them to try new things. Children feel especially happy when they sense that their parents have confidence in their ability to meet new challenges.
- Children are happy when they see their parents showing affection to each other.

A big part of every child's world is his family. A good family experience provides a child with the energy, stamina, and emotional foundation to strive to be bigger, better, and grown up.

School

Children constantly go back and forth between home and school throughout their childhood and teen years. However, children actually spend more waking hours in school than they do at home. So, for a child to be happy, school must be a positive experience.

- Children are happy when they are liked by other children and have friends in school.

- Children are happy when they are learning, passing tests, getting good grades, and have their projects displayed in school.
- Children are happy when their parents take an interest in their schooling, visit their classroom, know their teacher, and come to school events.
- Children are happy when the self-discipline they learned at home helps them to succeed in school. Self-disciplined children can make themselves work when they don't feel like working and will follow rules when they don't always feel like following rules.

Friends

Family and school are both important, but a child without friends will not grow. A child without friends is like a bird without wings. Friendships are crucial if children are to develop confidence, emotional maturity, and a connectedness to others.

- Children are happy when they are able to succeed at making and keeping friends.
- Children are happy when they can have friends visit their home to play and can sleep over at friends' houses.
- Children are happy when they know they are desired as playmates by other children.
- Children are happy when they have a variety of interests and skills so that friends find them interesting rather than boring.
- Children are happy when they have the social confi-

dence to follow rules while playing games and to tolerate not always being first and not always being the winner.

- Friends are important, but children always feel especially happy when they have a best friend. Best friends offer children a special kind of companionship where trust and support are honored.

Families, school, and friends make up a child's whole world and that is why parents need to ask themselves the following question each month:

"How is my child doing within the family, in school, and with her friends?"

Your answer to this question will determine if you have to intervene in any way on your child's behalf to ensure her continued progress and well-being. As you can see from this simple and easy strategy, a child feeling distant from a parent, failing in school, and with no friends is a child at risk for all sorts of emotional difficulties. The primary symptom alerting the parents that something is wrong will be the child's unhappiness.

Do you ever wonder why some families are happier than others—why some families have more success in life raising happy, well-adjusted children? Because of my practice, I have had the opportunity to compare thousands of families. I have observed that there are ten major differences between happy families and families who are unhappy.

THE TEN DIFFERENCES BETWEEN
HAPPY AND UNHAPPY FAMILIES

1. Happy Families Have Parents
Who Are Each Other's Cheerleader

In happy families we find that the adult partners validate each other as parents. They endorse each other to their children. This means that each parent communicates to the children that the other parent is a really good person and should be loved and respected. Each parent actually encourages the children to love, respect, obey, and admire the other parent.

In unhappy families parents tend to badmouth each other to their children. They each communicate to their children the faults of the other parent. And in this way they undermine each other's authority with the children.

2. Happy Families Value the Extended Family

Happy families stay connected with their relatives. They communicate and plan get-togethers with grandparents, aunts, uncles, nieces, and nephews, no matter where they live.

Unhappy families lose touch with their families of origin. The children are uncertain of who their relatives are, their names, their ages, and their careers. Family pride just doesn't seem to exist in unhappy families.

3. Happy Families Plan Fun

Happy families actually plan to have family fun together and set time aside for it. Families that do well value enjoying each other and build this into their family life.

Unhappy families never seem to have the time to enjoy each other. Plans for fun are rarely made in advance.

4. Happy Families Compliment Members of Their Family

In happy families family members compliment each other. They show appreciation to each other. The parents model this behavior and the children copy their parents. Compliments such as the following are often heard in happy families.

> "That was a great dinner."
> "Thanks for helping out."
> "What a wonderful idea."
> "You are so thoughtful."
> "Thanks for being such a good listener."
> "You look so nice in your new dress."

Unhappy families rarely take the time to give compliments to each other. Here is an interesting piece of research. It has even been found that the happier people are with their lives, the more compliments they give to others.

5. In Happy Families, Parents Watch Their Language

Happy families avoid abusive language. Happy families watch what they say to each other and how they say those things. They don't shoot from the hip and beat each other up with cutting words or sarcasm or swearing. If someone needs to be criticized, the criticism is not communicated in a way that insults the other family member.

In unhappy families the members say whatever comes to mind when they are upset. They are almost oblivious to how powerful and damaging words can be to the feelings and self-esteem of others in the family.

6. Parents Continue to Be a Couple

In happy families husbands and wives do not stop being a couple once they become a mother and a father. Parents, in other words, nurture their marriage. They seem to know instinctively that as the marriage goes, so goes the family. Time to get away as a couple is scheduled. Anniversaries are celebrated and partner's birthdays are honored.

I have found that in unhappy families, parents have a hard time balancing their roles as husband and wife with their roles as mother and father. Soon the parents are living parallel lives and putting their marriage second to the children.

7. Parents Avoid Holding Grudges

Successful families recognize and accept that getting angry with each other is normal. They know that people of different ages living under one roof are bound to get on each other's nerves now and then. So they are quick to forgive, forget, make up, and apologize. They don't hold onto grudges or their anger for hours and days.

In unhappy families, though, letting go of anger is so difficult. Family members pout and give other members the silent treatment or the cold shoulder for days.

8. Parents Follow Family Traditions

Happy families enjoy having traditions. Traditions are special ways of doing fun things at particular times of the year. In a sense, such traditions say to everyone in the family that this is how their family is unique. This is how we celebrate the holidays. This is how we spend our summer.

Unfortunately, unhappy families often lack traditions.

9. Parents Value Communication

The members of happy families talk to each other. They find time to have discussions and time to have family meetings. They listen to each other and they express their feelings to each other honestly, openly, but respectfully.

Unhappy families are more like emotional loners. These family members keep to themselves. They rarely express their feelings. And they seem not to be concerned if one family member is sad or upset. I always tell families that they must not ignore a member of the family who is unhappy. Something negative is going on and it most likely will affect the whole family in a bad way.

10. Parents Establish Rules and Consequences

In happy families the children know what is expected of them. Rules and consequences are clearly stated.

In unhappy families the children never seem to have a clear picture of what is expected of them and what the punishment will be if they break a rule. In these families, getting praised for just being good rarely happens. Rules remain vague and often are not consistently applied.

———

To summarize, happy families, more often than not, endorse each other as parents, give compliments, stay connected with relatives, are sensitive to how they say things to each other, do not hold grudges, enjoy family traditions, value communication, make time for fun, and structure their family life with rules and consequences for the children. When parents organize their family life around these values, they are more likely to raise children who are well adjusted and happy.

SEVENTEEN PARENTING GUIDELINES FOR EFFECTIVE PARENTING

The following parenting guidelines have helped many adults become more effective parents.

1. As you parent your children, be very aware that *you are your children's teacher.* This thought will keep you focused on teaching your children the many lessons of life they need to learn.
2. Think of your home as your classroom for teaching your children. This thought will remind you that a great deal of learning and training takes place right in your own household.
3. Keep in mind that your main mission is to raise chil-

dren who someday will be able to successfully run their own lives. This thought will help you to promote independence and resilience in your children.

4. Look for those times when your child spontaneously behaves the way you want him to behave. Then bring this behavior to your child's attention by praising him and by acknowledging how well he is doing. This thought will make you aware that there is a positive side to disciplining children and that discipline involves a lot of training and molding of behavior.

5. Be sure to make each child in your family an only child at least once a week. Children need private, one-on-one time with their parents. The parent who takes time for this experience will be rewarded by having fun times that are special each week and by having a more cooperative child.

6. Provide your child with feedback on what impact his behavior is having on others in the family. When parents take time to provide feedback, they are giving valuable information to the child on how his behavior has helped or hindered a brother or a sister or the parents themselves. This is one very important way children learn to become thoughtful to the needs of others and to behave appropriately.

7. Be very aware that the example you set by your own behavior will be the standard you set for your children, who are watching you. This thought will help you remember that, to your children, you are their role model. Children are great copycats, and by observing their parents they learn how a man behaves and how a

woman behaves and how married couples in love treat one another.

8. Structure your home with rules, consequences, routines, traditions, and expectations. This is called discipline. This thought will remind you that discipline at home helps children to develop self-discipline within themselves.

9. Avoid the frantic lifestyle so many American families now live. This thought will remind you to limit the number of outside enrichment experiences your children are signed up for and the number of commitments you personally make outside the family. The advice from child experts in the past that good parents can never do enough for their children is a trap leading to parents becoming overscheduled and overextended. It is also a trap that robs families of the time they need to just be a family.

10. Teach your child manners. A child with manners is a respectful child who is attractive to both peers and adults.

11. Raise your children to expect problems and to think of themselves as problem solvers. This thought will remind you that life is difficult and it is every parent's job to teach the children to cope and to seek solutions to the life problems they encounter.

12. Teach your children to work. Those families with a family business are in the easiest position to train their children to work. However, in this day and age every parent needs help in running the family and there is plenty of work to go around. Learning to work is one of the greatest lessons parents can teach a child. Chil-

dren need a work ethic and not a sense of entitlement that good things will just come their way without any effort on their part. Children around the age of two and a half to three love to be helpers. This is a great age to introduce your children to the idea that everyone in the family helps out and works for the benefit of all.

13. Avoid the materialism that has infected children today so badly; that what is valued most is what is still in the store. Teaching children that happiness relates to how much you own is a false value. It is a lesson that sets up an addiction for buying things.

14. Keep in mind that parenting is not a popularity contest. Many of your decisions will be unpopular with your children, but that is all right. You know what is best for your children. Stay focused on your ultimate goal as a parent—to prepare your children to live on their own.

15. Don't always rescue your children from their mistakes. Some of the best lessons a child learns are those gleaned from their own mistakes. Mistakes are inevitable, and they are opportunities to do better. So don't always rush in and save your child from the consequences of his misdirected behavior, unless of course there is some danger involved.

16. Remain aware that you are not to become your child's servant. Parents start out as servants because infants, toddlers, and preschoolers are so dependent and needy. But from age three on, parents slowly need to do less while asking their children to do more.

17. Be sure to nurture thoughtfulness in your child. Lots of times a child will misbehave or bother someone and all the parent says is "stop that" or "come here" or "hey." These statements in no way inform a child what he or she did wrong. Give your children feedback in a loving way as to how their behavior created a problem or bothered someone else. This is how you build sensitivity and thoughtfulness in a child.

SUMMARY

You are a parent forever. When you have raised happy children, you will have both a lifetime of good memories and years of pleasure in relating to your children as adults. I hope the thoughts, experiences, and advice presented in this book will help you to raise the kind of children you always dreamed of having. HAPPY PARENTING!

RESOURCES

For more reading on this topic I recommend the following books and Web site:

Bad Childhood, Good Life, by Laura Schlessinger, PhD (New York: HarperCollins, 2006).

The Childhood Roots of Adult Happiness: Five Steps to Help Kids Create and Sustain Lifelong Joy, by Edward M. Hallowell, MD (New York: Ballantine Books, 2002).

How to Parent with Your Ex: Working Together for Your Child's Best Interest, by Brette McWhorter Sember (Naperville, IL: Sphinx, 2005).

How to Raise an Emotionally Healthy Happy Child, by Albert Ellis, PhD, with Sandra Moseley and Janet L. Wolfe, PhD (Hollywood, CA: Wilshire Book Company, 1966).

How to Raise Great Kids: The Six Essential Habits of Highly Successful Parents, by Alan Davidson, PhD, and Robert Davidson (New York: Warner Books, 1996).

Raising Children in a Socially Toxic Environment, by James Garbarino, PhD (San Francisco: Jossey-Bass, 1995).

What Children Learn from Their Parents' Marriage: It May Be Your Marriage, but It's Your Child's Blueprint for Intimacy, by Judith P. Siegel, PhD, CSW (New York: HarperCollins, 2000).

Why a Daughter Needs a Mom: 100 Reasons, by Gregory E. Lang (Nashville, TN: Cumberland House, 2003).

Why a Son Needs a Dad: 100 Reasons, by Gregory E. Lang (Nashville, TN: Cumberland House, 2003).

Why Marriages Succeed or Fail and How You Can Make Yours Last, by John Gottman, PhD, with Nan Silver (New York: Simon & Schuster, 1994).

You Are Your Child's First Teacher, by Rahima Baldwin Dancy (Berkeley, CA: Celestial Arts, 2000).

http://www.aap.org/, American Academy of Pediatrics Web site.

INDEX